Mahalekshmi Manoj

Mahalekshmi Manoj who works in Al Jalila Children's Hospital, Dubai as Medical Secretary resides in Sharjah with her husband and daughter and hails from Thiruvananthapuram, Kerala. "Fragrance of Memories" is her third book.

English Language
Fragrance of Memories
(Memories)
by
Mahalekshmi Manoj
Translated by
Dr. M.V. Mukundan

Published in October 2023
Second Impression December 2023
by Decan Imprint Publishing Co.
Reg. Off: Sharjah Publishing City
Free Zone Sharjah, UAE.
Phone: 00971-551830334
Email : decanimprint@gmail.com

Cover Design : Prasanth Mangad

Printed at
Manipal Technologies Ltd.

03/23-24/Sl.No.03/100/NS 15.4
ISBN 978-93-5973-037-0

Fragrance of Memories

Mahalekshmi Manoj

DECANIMPRINT

Dedication

To my mother, who made me who I am today, by crossing the path of life alone which were full of stones and thorns.

To my husband, who supports me in everything and helped my dreams grow wings and fly.

To my sister, my Chinnu, who always stands as a shadow in crisis.

To my dear and beloved friends Vidya and Deepa who is protecting me from rain and sun throughout my life with the umbrella of deep friendship, and who distinguishes me from right and wrong since the time I started writing.

To Soja and Renu, my sisters from another mother.

To Mridula, who loves me and always prays for the best to happen for me since the day we met.

To the Lord who showers all these blessings on me.

Introduction

"There is no use of you studying anything", when the night a relative said these words to me while I was studying, out of grief, I punched something, initial writings that could be called mine, I tore up what I had written and threw in the trash, and then several diary entries, which were also left as scraps of paper in various forms.

Reading was and still is an addiction to me. There was a time when I searched out and read even small paper cuttings, but now reading is only during times when I could call "me time", because of the hustle and bustle of expatriate life.

It is only in recent times that writings have begun to take the form of stories. I will be the only one who would name me as a "story writer" as I come from a family that doesn't have any claim of writing.

The belief that a book would come out in my name was so far-fetched that I, like any writer, wished and even prayed for a book of my stories to come out.

It is through social media platforms that everything I wrote and kept came into light as stories. This is now going to be in book form for my love relationships, soulmates and dear friends who love me and my writing.

About half of the stories in this book's characters are none other than me and includes my life's paths which were a mix of bitter and sweet. "The Fragrance of Memories" is a combination of thirty-eight years of my experiences and life stories of people whom I have met or heard.

Index

Stories Written from Life

"Fragrance of Memories" is a beautiful short story collection by Mahalekshmi Manoj, an upcoming Dubai based writer, whose stories have been widely accepted on the online platform for the last 2 years. Being an expat and a hospital professional, most of her stories reflect the heartbeats of an expatriate and are sewn by the threads of a hospital background. Through her little stories, Mahalekshmi lifts the readers to the various aura of love, friendship, kindness, grief, sorrow, kinship, consideration and above all the goodness of heart.

As the author herself has quoted, these stories themselves have found their origin from the pages of her own life; the female characters are a replica of her own image depicting the bitter experiences of her childhood and the strenuous path she has walked through, yet the reader is given to the satisfaction that life has kept aside some memorable fragrance too…

A fact worth-mentioning is the simple, common place vocabulary maintained by the author all the way through by which the reader connects with the events, atmosphere and the characters.

A pen journey that take the readers by the hand through very simple yet powerful emotions, inflicting a sense of bliss within - that is where "Fragrance of Memories" leave us till the last leaf.

Saividya Ambikapathy

Bosom Friend

Yamuna sat looking at the overflowing water in different directions from the chasm which is formed on the un-cemented road in front of her house because of the heavy rainfall which began yesterday. Only one more week is left for the reopening of schools. Normally, it was customary that the rains start pouring on the school reopening day.

Yamuna couldn't find any sign of a sudden abatement in the rain falling. Though it is a pleasant experience to watch and to feel the coldness of rain, this sixth class student was disturbed by some other thoughts. In place of that beautiful scenario, Yamuna was haunted by a bigger problem pertaining to her age group.

She was using the same school bag for the last three years. She was neither worried about the years nor the oldness, but her school bag was totally worn and she couldn't do no more stitching on that material, so she used some safety pins to keep the school bag somewhat intact and is intending for further use.

The condition of her school bag was same during the school closing days and she was not able to use it as a back-pack then. When she tries to do so, the stitches rip apart and keeps the bag's mouth wide open. So she kept her bag always close to her chest. Some of her classmates even ridiculed her in this regard. However, this being a common practice, Yamuna sat in the class with no negative emotions, as if she was in no way affected by those comments.

Nevertheless, bringing the same worn bag to the class is unimaginable to her. Mom has already intimated her that she was not in a capacity to buy Yamuna a new school bag. Yamuna has already repaired her torn sandals and has taken a decision to use the same for some more days, but, the bag; in that coldness of the rain, she thought over and over about it and she was totally disturbed.

Actually, three years ago her father only bought that bag for her. That year itself, her father left this world after he met with an accident. Along with his life, the hopes and dreams of Yamuna and her mother flew away. They were literally drawn to destitution. Yamuna recalled those good old days with her father and thought about the miseries of her family in his absence.

This morning, when she woke up, she saw her mother replacing some Aluminium utensils kept here and there inside their house. They were kept in order to collect the rainwater falling inside, from above the dilapidated roof.

Though she nodded to the routine instructions of her mother who was in a hurry to reach her work place, Yamuna's apprehensions revolved around the sewed up school bag that was kept on the little table. It was the last gift from her beloved father. Thus she has an invaluable intimacy towards that school bag. Actually, her mother is waiting for a monthly subscription lottery to be availed. She is waiting for that money to receive in order to replace the broken roofing – tiles. At the same time, Yamuna was expecting to buy a new school bag from that money. Hearing her mother's plan, Yamuna once again felt very much dissatisfied. She lost her expectations.

During the day time, Yamuna went to Arunima's house. She is her uncle's daughter and is of the same age. While playing with her, Yamuna realised that her first cousin and her parents will go for a shopping that evening. Arunima will get new school bag, umbrella and sandals! The rainfall stopped for a while. There felt a small relief. The sun peeped above the dark clouds and shone. It was a pleasant seen and it lit a small wick in the lamp of expectation sprouted in the innocent heart of the little girl, a ray of hope! "Maybe, they will buy a bag for me too". She prayed with mental agony that may God prompt them to buy one for her too.

That evening, Yamuna sat at the corridor and was eagerly waiting for the return of her cousin's family after shopping. They returned very late. Yamuna didn't have her food even. Her mother insisted her to eat her dinner. "I will have it later, mom", she said. Her eyes were on the road.

Yamuna saw the light beams of her cousin's vehicle from afar and her heart started to throb strongly. Though it was late night, she entered into their house. Arunima was enthusiastically taking out all the materials bought on that evening and was removing their covers. She showed all the new items very happily to Yamuna. Arunima was very much excited and was caressing them and enjoyed the new smell and beauty. When Arunima's mom came towards them, Yamuna asked, "Where is my bag, Auntie?". Her mindset by now has convinced her that they certainly would have bought a bag for her too. Her expectation has become a confirmation, that confirmation only made her ask such a question.

"What?"…."Bag for you?" …."Did your mom handover us money for the same?" …"Really interesting…what a beautiful expectation!" the flow of such contemptuous words pierced into that little girl's heart as thorns. Those sharp words literally dissected her little heart. Before the rolling tears fell down, she stood up and slowly went out of that furnace of defamation.

While entering into her house, she took much caution to hide from her mom any kind of inner pressure reflecting on her face. Her mom told her: "Tonight also it's raining cats and dogs. I have to put more utensils to collect water. Otherwise, the entire house will be filled with water. Yamuna, have some food and go to bed."

Yamuna's mother did only see the rain pouring outside, she didn't see the rain of insult and pain pouring inside her daughter's mind. Yamuna considered it as a good thing. If happened to know, that will certainly hurt her mom.

Next week, the school re-opened. On the reopening day, Yamuna entered her classroom with the stale bag close to her chest. She found her friends showing their new bags, umbrellas and sandals each other and sharing their happiness. She sat lonely on a bench. Yamuna was waiting for the arrival of Nanditha who used to be her only close and loving friend.

When got promotion to class seven from sixth, the only one thing Yamuna enquired was that, whether Nanditha is in the same class.

When got confirmation in this regard, Yamuna sighed with relief. From class one onwards, they were shadows to each other. Nandu also would have bought new items, she thought.

Yamuna came out of her imaginary world, when Nandu put her hands on her shoulders. Yamuna was shocked to see the old bag again in Nandu's hands. "What Nandu, didn't you buy a new bag this year?"

"Of course, bought new bag, sandals and umbrella, not only for me..., for you too!". "Oh, for me too?", Yamuna got excited with extreme happiness.

"Yes dear, everything bought for you too. The bags are alike, but different in colour. Since you like pink colour most, bought one with that colour for you. Last week, my dad decided to go for the purchase. Then I told him that I don't need anything this year, but buy things for Yamuna. Then my dad offered to buy things for both of us. Actually, my mom and I were planning to visit your home yesterday to give you a surprise, unfortunately we were not able to make it. Don't worry, we will visit you this evening. We can use the new items tomorrow onwards, ok?"

Nanditha raised her palm to high-five with Yamuna's. Yamuna slowly removed her palm and kissed Nandu on her cheek, with eyes filled with tears of happiness.

When she looked out through the classroom windows, she could see the dark clouds forming a bank in the sky, but her mind was on cloud nine, just like a shining sky without any dark clouds.

That evening, Yamuna sat on the corridor, much excitedly waiting for the arrival of her dearest friend. When she saw her best friend with her mother walking towards her house, her enthusiasm and happiness reached the apex.

Yamuna learnt the great lesson about the importance of sharing to the needy on that day. She imbibed the most important humanistic value that it is important to share from your possessions, basically, from her ever-loving friendship.

The most memorable and beautiful moment of Yamuna's life bloomed in this bud of friendship.

Human

"Dr. Peter did you notice there?".

As a reply to the question, "Why you had never moved from this small clinic to a larger room during your thirty-five years of service?", asked by young doctor, Dr. Peter, who had just joined a famous cancer center for children in New York, Dr. Alexander who is the head of the Department and the favourite doctor to the kids asked.

Dr. Peter turned his gaze to where Dr. Alexander pointed, the vast greenery beyond the glass windows of Dr. Alexander's room. He saw a huge tree. Dr. Peter felt that there was something special about that tree, but he was not clear what it was, so he looked at Dr. Alexander questioningly.

"Look at that tree, doesn't it look like a wooden statue of Saint Anthony?'.

Dr. Peter looked again in amazement at the wooden statue of Saint Anthony holding a baby in his arms, with the right branch leaning forward and the left branch bending inwards.

"The tree has been here since I joined this hospital and when I am on my seat it feels like Saint Anthony is standing in front of me. It is not made by any human being, but by nature, i.e. God, the creator of all living beings. For that reason alone, I decided that even though the buildings, office and rooms of this cancer center are big, this room is enough for me. I have only requested two things from the hospital management till today, one, I want this room till I leave here, the children will be consulted here, and two, there should be nothing beyond these glass windows to cover that tree. I have a faith that he will take care of the children who comes to me with illness."

"Doctor you are so godly, then why isn't there even a picture of the gods in this room?", Dr. Peter asked again.

"Why put a lifeless picture when nature itself has placed Saint Anthony in front of me?", Dr. Alexander said looking at the tree.

"Didn't you ever feel that you should stop working and enjoy retirement?".

"How can I rest when the babies are sick? I believe that God has sent me here to help them. My retirement will only happen after my death. I always pray to Saint Anthony that I should be able to take care of the sick babies until my last breath."

"Can you tell me doctor what has given you joy as well as sorrow during your long service?".

"The only thing that makes me happy then and now is when I tell the parents of a baby, 'Your kid's biopsy results are benign'. The happiness in their eyes when they hear that is my joy and the satisfaction I get from this service. Sadness: Two things, one being told "your baby's biopsy result is malignant" and two being told "your baby is no more". In all these years of being a doctor, I have faced six times the fateful moment when I bowed my head and said, "Your baby is no more." As I walked up to those parents to tell them the sad news, I wished that I had died before I got there so that I could have left this world without telling them the saddest news, or that I had died before those babies' death. If any of the kids I treated pass away, I would go to Saint Anthony's Church on that day and pray for their souls. I'm sure I'll meet them someday on another beautiful shore, but I'm afraid when they see me there, they will ask me, "Why did you leave us to death?", whether they would fight with me?, whether they would be angry with me, but I also hope that they would invite me in by saying, "Let it go, it doesn't matter, you come in." Rather than being a doctor or the head of such a big hospital, I am a simple human, seeing the pains and difficulties of children as my own, and moving forward believing that nothing will happen to them and God will take care of them. When they laugh, I also laugh along with them but when they cry, I cry on their back."

Dr. Alexander looked at the wooden statue of Saint Anthony and said these to Dr. Peter. Both of their eyes were filled with tears. It became clear to Dr. Peter why Dr. Alexander is the favourite doctor of the children who come here for treatment.

Dr. Peter was happy to learn from Dr. Alexander that being a good doctor means to have a place with the gods in the minds of the patients.

While Dr. Peter was walking out of Dr. Alexander's room, Dr. Alexander was looking at the biopsy result of a nine-year-old kid and seeing the result as benign, he thankfully looked at the greenery beyond the glass windows, to the huge tree with the shape of Saint Anthony.

Courtesy

"Sister, how are you?"

Though five months have passed since my arrival in Sharjah, my job in this hospital began two weeks ago only. My job was in the I.C. unit. As the security staff sitting adjacent to me was a Malayali, my job went very smoothly without any mental struggle.

During the beginning of the third week, I saw a stout, well-built, black man in the place of the Malayali security staff. I felt a little bit puzzled. I didn't answer the question he asked, when I heard the thick-accented words. I shivered with fear.

'Hello sister, I am Charles, the newly appointed security here." He extended his hands from the long cabin, opposite to my seat. Once again, I trembled.

I ogled around to see whether there is somebody to help me out, but to my disappointment I couldn't find any one, "I am Maha, ..Mahalakshmi, I.C.U. Secretary", I replied and shook his hands with little shiver.

"I am from Nigeria, and hope you are from India."

"Yes, India", I gave him the reply without looking at him. I was praying to the God to help me, because I have heard about the fraudulence and robbery done by the Nigerians before.

My colleagues belonging to other wards used to call me, Mahi. Charles too, started to call me Sister Mahi and gradually my tensions started to melt down.

Most of the bystanders of the patients were reluctant to speak with Charles, because of his size and appearance. They used to approach me for permission to enter into the I.C.U. Though, I personally had the permission to enter, I didn't have the right to allow bystanders. Most of the time, I was put in a dilemma on such occasions, to answer them.

"I am the security in charge here. You need to take my permission to enter into the I.C.U. Sister is busy with her jobs. Don't disturb her, please.", he told the patient's bystanders. This way he helped me on many occasions.

We were going through high degree of financial strains during that time. Once in a week, that too on Thursdays only we bought the indispensable things. Those days, we never had anything called needs or favorites, it was only necessities. We used to limit the purchase to a maximum of 100 or 150 dirhams. It was a time when we were too cautious to avoid the loss of even a single dirham. Meanwhile, my relationship with Charles grew to that of a more cordial one. He used to ask about my daughter and I surprisingly started to realize his good heart inside the huge body.

I used to keep the 100 dirhams along with the list of items to buy with that money, in an inner lining of my office handbag on Wednesday itself. Friday being a holiday, I used to buy groceries on Thursday evenings, and went back home on foot. On that particular Thursday, I searched for the money and list, to keep in my coat's pocket. I was shocked to see that the money was missing. I spread out all the things from my bag on the table, but couldn't find the money and list. I felt dizzy and sat on the chair. My eyes were filled with tears.

"Where did the money go" How will I purchase groceries? What will I tell to my husband?". He won't criticize me, I know. But I knew only very well that it would be another struggle for him to find ways to obtain the same amount. All these worries increased my sadness and I wanted to cry loudly. At this moment, Charles approached me and asked me what's going on.

Actually, he noticed my agitated state of mind, but I got irritated. I confirmed in my mind that, Charles had taken my money in my absence, during the one-hour break. "My 100 dirhams is lost", I told in a faint voice. Actually, I became more exhausted, rather than being angry with him. I got upset because of the loss of money and helplessness to buy our needy things.

"Where did you keep the money, Sister?"

"Here.", Even though I doubted him, I answered and showed him the small chamber with zip inside the bag. At the same time, I was aware of the fact that he was the only person to support me at that moment.

"Sister Mahi, the chamber has got a small slit underneath. Maybe, the money has gone inside that tearing. Can you look?"

I snatched the bag from his hand with trepidation, but with full vigor and put my fingers into the slit and searched. I felt touching some paper like thing and in a helter–skelter way, I took it out. It was my 100 dirhams, which I thought as lost and being taken by Charles.

If Charles hadn't found it for me, I would have been so depressed in the thought that it was lost, and our weekend, which we found so much joy in our own little privacy, would have been spoiled thinking about this loss.

Soon Charles got another job and when he said goodbye, my heart was aching as if someone dear to me had left my life forever.

Apart from a handful of blood relations, I owe my life to people like Charles. My little life on many occasions was made beautiful and happy being surrounded by people like them.

The Joys of Time

Chinara, who is an Ethiopian lady, was my colleague in the hospital where I started my job in this foreign country. Her husband also lived here. Their single daughter, meanwhile, lived with Chinara's sister in an Ethiopian village.

Chinara was a helper in the hospital and her husband was a delivery boy in one of the K.F.C. outlets. They got very meager salary.

Chinara is a well-educated lady. She was very proud to tell me that she is the most educated lady in her village. However, lack of experience in the field of her studies put her in this situation to take up the job of a helper. She is very fluent in English language, and showed the same talent in learning Arabic too. She used to talk to the Arab patients legibly without any inhibition.

From the conversation with her, I have understood that the culture of Ethiopia is almost as same as ours (Keralites). During off-duty time, she dressed in a gentle way. She used to be very different from other African nationals and always talked in a noble style.

Chinara and her husband were neighbors and they got married after falling in love. As same as other employees working here, she also came here as a breadwinner, and earnestly wished to bring her daughter here, but the salary of both the wife and husband was not enough to fulfill her wish. So she started to search for a better job in Dubai, from the very beginning. She was very confident in her capabilities. I always saw her filled with confidence, happy and optimistic.

One day when I went for my duty, a very different Chinara welcomed me. She looked very sad with reddened eyes just opposite to that of her usual pleasantness. Her grief was such that no woman could bear it, and she cried bitterly and told that her husband has been having an extra-marital affair and that was the basis for her sadness. He doesn't like her anymore and he openly told that he liked the other woman. Chinara told me this issue and began to cry. I groped for words to convince her. I could only be empathetic to her.

Maybe it is only a misconception among some of us that we Indians are the only people who value relationships. In fact, nowadays our perception as regards to relationships have changed a lot. When I saw Chinara's sorrowful condition, such thoughts of mine got buried up somewhere.

Their problems continued as such. Chinara bid goodbye from there with a firm conviction that everything will get settled within one or two months. I was fully confident about her capabilities.

Years and seasons continued their race just as the trees shed their leaves. Terrible heat was replaced by biting cold, and hot wind gave way to cool breeze. Chinara went into my deepest memory, sometimes I recalled her. Five years have passed by.

During a winter evening, while I was walking to my home with wild thoughts, a pure white car came rushing and stopped suddenly very near to me. I was really surprised to see the person coming out of the driving seat. My mind got filled with happiness. I forgot myself for a moment.

It was Chinara! She came to me and hugged me. "Let me give you a surprise, Maha", she said. Opening the side door, she brought out a girl. It was her daughter, Charity.

She continued. "I have brought her here, dear. She is studying in Grade 3, in a school in Dubai. Now, I am working in a good company in Dubai, as Financial Advisor. See…, I took driving license and now I have a car." She seemed to be very excited.

I was happy, surprised, and moreover proud. I thought about her growth. I hugged her daughter and said, I am so….so happy for you." Then I doubtfully enquired about her husband.

"We are divorced now, Maha. He still works in K.F.C. Last month, you know…, we had a party in my office and I sponsored it. He was the one who delivered the order and I paid the amount with my head held high."

"Do we call this sort of instances as sweet revenge?" I just aired this question to her.

She replied, "Maha, frankly, I did not feel any sweet revenge. In my heart, I still have the real love towards him, and it will be there forever. He surely has a place in my heart, but not in my life anymore. Let God strengthen him."

She never implored before her husband that he should not forsake her. She was quite clear that love can't be seized by force. I was never surprised in her deeds. I was sure that, a lady like Chinara, who is having much integrity will always manage things in such a way.

She compelled me to spend some time with her and she took me to a juice shop and bore the expenses. She said that, it was her right to do so. Once again, I was not able to refuse her affection and invitation. Spending some time with her gave me a lot of happiness and pride.

The past and present conditions in Chinara's life once again confirmed my faith that God will always be there to support the neglected ones. Moreover, when we love somebody unconditionally, we can't hate them ever. This faith also is substantiated by Chinara's behavior, because she never showed any kind of grudge towards her husband.

After bidding goodbye to the mother and daughter, I returned home. My mind was as cool as the outside breeze during the winter. Also, I assured them that we will meet again. My heart was throbbing with immense happiness, after a long time.

Seeing our beloved person, who in turn loves us unconditionally, overcoming his/her difficult condition and landing safely in the comfort zone gives us indescribable happiness, is'nt that a sheer luck!

Angel

"Sister, can you give me some water?".

I asked the nurse who was near me when I was lying down after the caesarean section, and although I did not feel the pain because of the numbness, I was thirsty, and I felt that I couldn't hold it any longer because of the fatigue.

"You can't drink water now. I'll give you tomorrow. If you drink water, you'll feel uncomfortable and also throw up. You have to be careful with the stitch. I'll soak this cotton in water and wet your lips in between, then you'll get some relief."

While moistening my lips with cotton, sister said very compassionately, but when I heard that, I felt very sad of not getting water, it is true there is no other thing as precious as water.

The lady in the next bed had normal delivery. When her pain had increased, her cries also became louder, and I had also cried seeing her husband who was in tears standing right next to her. I had never felt such a hunger for food and water when I saw her family giving her bread and black tea. Watching all these, I lay on my head, thinking that there was no one near me.

The nurse who understood my distress came close to me and patted my hands, she told;

"It doesn't matter, you know, if you talk too much, the stitch will come out, that's why doctor told everyone to stay out. The situation will change soon, tomorrow will be the same as before. Your husband is working outside the country?, he couldn't come? I was like this too, my husband was not around us during both deliveries. I can understand Lakshmi's pain." Seeing a small bruise near the palm of her right hand, which was red, I slowly asked,

"What happened to your palm sister?"

"You did everything and you are asking me what happened?", a response came from the sister accompanied by laughter.

When the team put me on the caesarean table, held me down, gave an injection in my spine, made an incision in my abdomen and tried to get the baby out, I was struggling to breathe, out of frenzy that I may die, I clutched the right hand of the sister who stood near me and dug my nails into it. It was only after the baby was taken out that I was able to breathe and I released the grip on her arm and then let go. Even while half conscious, I came to know that she did not try to free her palm from my clutch.

That little bruise was the cut made by my fingernails. I was at a loss as to what to reply, and could do nothing but looked miserably at her face and at the bruise in her palm.

"I didn't free my hand, I thought it would be comforting to you, I have also suffered the same pain and struggle. My wound will be healed by the time you get up and walk."

I didn't have to think twice to associate the name of the sister with her kind words, looks and touch as an angel.

Success Of Life

"Hello, good morning Dr. Daniel, I am the class teacher of your son, Philip. Please come to our school at 9 am tomorrow. I know that you are a busy surgeon, but at any cost, you must come to the school, so, see you tomorrow, doctor."

Dr. Daniel is a prominent surgeon in a well-known child hospital in the country. He is endeared by children, their parents, and his colleagues equally, because of his behavior as well as proficiency. He loved everyone around him. Disregard of their positions, he behaved politely with everyone. Thus he is an odd man out among other doctors in that hospital.

While examining a two-year-old girl's curly toes, Dr. Daniel received a phone call from his youngest son Philip's class teacher. Normally doctor doesn't answer phone calls when he's examining children, but when he saw "Philip's class teacher calling" he couldn't help but pick up.

Philip is the youngest of his three children. Two elder girls are outstanding in studies and co-curricular activities, but Philip is a little bit backward in this regard. He is an average student, a little mischievous and aggressive in nature. Within these ten years, he has committed numerous mischiefs. Almost on all days, his mother received phone calls from the school, highlighting his misbehavior or guilt.

Dr. Daniel and his wife Teena nurtured their children by providing them essential freedom and opportunities to take free stands. They never punished them beyond a limit, even if they committed grave mistakes. They never gave severe punishment or used hurting words. They told them that they are free to make silly mischiefs, instead, they insisted them not to hurt anybody in any case. They instructed them to give equal weightage in sharing the distress as well as pleasure among their friends. They strictly insisted them to earmark some time for prayers daily.

When compared with the elder girls, Philip was a little more mischievous and childish, but he was never a notorious boy. The doctor and his wife, till date, have never noticed or heard a hurtful act done by Philip towards others. Why did the teacher summoned me to the school? Thinking like this, the doctor massaged the toes of the two year old girl who was sitting in front of him. The cute girl presented a sweet laugh, showing her single milk tooth, each on both jaws, as if she got tickled by the doctor. Watching it, the doctor became cool and came out of his thoughtful mind, which was covered with black clouds. There is no other valuable medicine than the laughter of kids in bringing back a badly affected mind to normality, Dr. Daniel often told this to his colleagues.

"Daddy, did Victoria madam give you a call?, did she ask you to come to the school tomorrow?". When Dr. Daniel reached home after duty, his son asked him, before the doctor enquiring about the same.

"Sure, she did call. My son, you may be sure that I am very busy nowadays. Nevertheless, I have to come. Your class teacher insisted to do so. What is the problem for today?

"To be frank, I don't know, Daddy."

The doctor once again became anxious. What may be the mistake that Philip committed, of which he himself is unaware of? Mrs. Teena was standing near to them, thinking in the same way. Doctor gave a blink to her, to convince her that there is nothing to worry.

Next morning, both Dr. Daniel and Teena reached the school and were waiting for the class teacher in the reception. They heard one mother rebuking her daughter openly, in front of others.

"You come home this evening. The balance, I will give you there.", that woman trembled with anger. The worried daughter stood there helplessly, with full of tears in her eyes. Dr. Daniel, who is father of two girls and also a child specialist, sat there with utmost sadness, what may be the mistake did by that girl? Did she get very low mark in the exam? Or didn't listen to the class? Or any other silly matter like those? But is this the punishment for such things? Is this the way to punish her? Will the mental shock affected to the girl get cured any time? The doctor recalled the advice he used to give the parents of small children coming for the consultation, "It is not the marks they scored in the examinations which determine the success of their life, it is the values that we have to adhere in life to be considered as most important". Actually, counseling has to be initially executed to the parents who hurt the minds of their children. While thinking so, the class teacher invited them to the Principal's room.

"Welcome, Dr. Daniel and family". They heard this salutation with grand applause when they entered in to the room. They saw Philip standing in the midst of a group of teachers and students. At the first instance, they doubted a bit, but the prolonged applause gradually dissolved their anxiety.

"Dr. Daniel and Teena, your son Philip is the 'Super Star of the Month', and you wanted to know, how? He was present everywhere during the sports meet conducted in previous weeks.". Hearing the words of the Principal, the doctor and his wife looked at each other. They thought of Philip telling them not getting into the final rounds of sports meet.

"Doctor, what you thought is right. This recognition is not for his winning, it is on behalf of his contribution of prompts to other children. He encouraged the participants with boisterous shouting and excitement, which provided them great energy. Even in rounds in which he was not expelled, he prompted others. He served them with water and helped them in many ways. He motivated them continuously. We never saw any other student acting like him, so there was no other option for us to choose any one instead for Philip, to become the "Superstar of this Month.". Although he is just ten years old, the amount of caring he showed, his good character, and his success are all due to you, Doctor. He told us that his daddy only taught all these things to him and his sisters. Philip told us that you have taught them that there is no other happiness in this world greater than the happiness that we receive out of helping others. As a wonderful father and as a dedicated child specialist, you deserve his victory, Dr. Daniel."

While receiving the certificate along with Philip, the doctor felt much proud about his son. Dr. Daniel thanked his mother in his mind.

"Dear Dany, try to share the happiness as well as sorrows of others. Prompt people to do good things. Always think as if you are standing on their side. Don't do anything which the Almighty doesn't like. Find some time for prayers daily. If we can follow all these norms, we can make it sure that we have succeeded in our life. All the other things will be provided by the Almighty. He won't consider any of your possessions or richness when you die. If he happened to ask you a question, How did you spend your life for others?, at least we should have a specific answer which is true." These were his mother's words. Those words re-echoed in his ears. Yes, his son's success is actually the privilege of his mother.

Doctor lifted up Philip and put him on his shoulders. The cheers inside that room still continued.

The Little Teachers

I was waiting for the cab outside the hospital, literally exhausted after the day's work. Meanwhile I was thinking about tomorrow's pending work, and also about the things to do after reaching home. My mind was very much disturbed.

When we stand outside the hospital, the site of Burj Khalifa, the tallest building in the world, is visible afar. Since it being a hospital for children, many kids were moving hither and thither either with their mothers or caretakers, but all my attention was to see whether the cab is coming or not.

I was starting to feel more and more uneasy as the time for the cab to arrive was ticking away when I heard a baby's voice, "Hi, hello, how are you?".

I looked towards where I heard the noise and saw a boy, who appeared less than five years old, in a small cloth stroller.

I could tell at a glance that his legs were too small and his head was bigger than normal children, but the sparkle in his eyes was reflected in his face. When he asked me this question, he was looking inside for a second, and I thought he must be looking for his mother.

He, repeated the question, believing that either I didn't hear him, or for not getting an answer from me,

"Hi, hello, how are you?"

I slowly bend towards him and said, "I am good. How about you?"

"Me too. Are you okay?".

What surprised me more than his first question was his second question, "Are you okay?".

A boy, around five, and having a whole lot of physical uneasiness, asking to an elderly person in a sweet and kind-hearted way. I wondered whether anybody else had asked me such a question before in this sort of consoling way.

I replied. "I am okay my dear, thank you for your kindness."

Instantly, he replied, "It's ok, Take care."

Before I could say anything, his nanny came and pushed the stroller he was in and went inside. I just looked at the shining face moving, and meanwhile I received the missed call, as regards the arrival of the cab.

All the way back home, that little face was the only thing in my mind. His bright eyes and flowing copper hair tossed and tossed in my mind. I prayed for him all that time. Maybe, God himself might have brought him before me, to ease my tensions.

I felt like God asking me:

"Do you think that your problems are severe than his physical uneasiness? Never. You never show the degree of positivity in your life, which that little boy shows towards his life."

My whole thought was about the virtue I received from being able to meet him and even to talk to him. May the Lord bless that baby with all kinds of blessings.

Crowded with big men full of negativity, look around and you will see at least one baby face full of positivity, as I have seen.

They are the ones who actually teach us, the teachers who are small in body and very big in mind.

Heaven - Where Mother Is

"Anu, today is my daughter's birthday. I will arrange the lunch.", While joining the duty in the morning, Sneha told her colleague, Anupama.

"Oh, is it? Then why didn't you mention it earlier. At least, I would have bought some sweets for her."

Sneha laughed and said, "I don't want you to buy anything. That's why I didn't mention about it earlier."

"Oh, what's there in buying? She is only a small girl. Moreover, it's a pleasure."

"Its ok Anu, we can buy something from a restaurant in Karama. You just make a plan. I will meet the C.E.O. and come back." Sneha took the needed files and came out of the cabin.

There was a long corridor after their office space. It was always free. Since it was adjacent to their office space, only the hospital employees used it. The hospital I.C.U. and the N.I.C.U are just near and opposite to the corridor. The hospital was for children. Along the waiting area, we could see only parents or relatives of the children, in prayerful mood.

Sneha's office was attached to both the I.C.U. and the N.I.C.U. and she has got the access to enter into the department. But, in order to avoid seeing the painful scenes, she seldom used to go there.

While crossing the corridor, Sneha heard a 'Hi' in low voice. She stopped and looked to see who it was. On her left side, she saw a smiling little girl to her surprise. She removed her mask and laughed at that blue eyed cutie. She might be around six years, just the age of her daughter. How come she be there?, Sneha began to think.

"How did you come here, dear?" Sneha asked that girl, with golden skin and an enticing smile on her face. Sneha put her files on the floor, stood on her knees, and asked the little girl in a comfortable way. She looked around to see whether there is any of her relatives nearby. Sneha couldn't see any one. The time is only seven thirty, and employees are just arriving. By eight thirty, the office area will become live.

"I am here only." The child said.

"Where?"

"See, there!"

When the kid pointed to the I.C.U., Sneha asked her, " Your father or mother? Who works here?"

"Today is my birthday", she said, without giving an answer to Sneha's question.

"Oh, Is it this Cutie's birthday, today?". Today is the birthday of my daughter, too." "What's your name?", embracing her, I asked her the second question.

"Mariam Isa."

"What a beautiful name!"

"My mom named me."

"Where's your mom then?" "How come you be alone here?" " Won't your mother get panic?"

"I am here for the last six months. My mom died six months ago. She got drowned in the water. Aunty, do you know why we are not able to breathe inside the water?" Pointing towards the I.C.U, Mariam asked. Sneha literally got upset.

"Where's your Pappa? Come…., Aunty will take you".

"Pappa is not here. He got married with another Mom. Do you know Aunty?, Pappa only drowned us in water. That's how my Mom died."

"Drowned in water? ….and nothing happened to you?

"Sneha…", she heard Anupama calling from a distance, and looked to that direction. She was really shocked and wanted to ask many more questions to the kid.

"Dear, you stay here. Aunty will come back soon and then I will take you there."

"Will you pray for me, Aunty? I want to see my Mom. If all of us pray, Mom will come. Mamma used to tell that prayers can do wonders and miracles." Sneha was trying to go towards Anupama, but she came back to Mariam, who was standing there with filled eyes, and hugged the kid with heavy grief.

"I will pray, dear. Your Mom will come back to see you. You be here only. Aunty will be back soon."

While walking towards Anupama after asking the kid to stay there, Sneha started to pray: "Oh, God, there is nothing impossible for you in this world. Please her mother should come to the kid in her dreams to greet her birthday".

"What happened to you? I saw you sitting on your knees!"

"Didn't you see that kid? Somehow she came here. I was trying to understand her whereabouts. I asked her to stay there. Poor girl…., her mother….."

"What are you saying? Which kid? I didn't see anybody. I saw you, alone, showing some gestures and actions. What happened to you this morning?" Sneha got stuck there, hearing these words.

"Didn't you see me talking with the little kid?" Sneha was not at all convinced, and asked Anupama.

"No, never. What happened to you? I was calling you to get this paper signed." When she heard this, Sneha snatched that paper and hurried back to the corridor. She couldn't see Mariam there. She took the file she kept on the floor and walked ahead. She searched for Mariam in many places. Finally she was disappointed. She got signatures of the C.E.O. in the papers and returned to her office. One hour has passed by then. She has got a whole lot of questions as regards to Mariam. She longed to see the girl once more.

"Sneha, you had a call from Dr. Sathya from the I.C.U. Do you know, the patient in bed number two is no more. You should prepare the medical report urgently. That kid was in the ventilator, for the last six months, poor kid! Actually, she and her mom were drowned together. Mother lost her life instantly. The kid was brain dead. Now, she had a cardiac arrest. Her father never allowed to remove the ventilator. There may be case against the guardian for carelessness. Here in this country, that is the law, right?." When Sneha came back to her seat, Anupama told her. At that moment, Sneha felt uncontrolled heartbeats.

"What's the name of the patient?", she asked in a shivery voice.

"Mariam Isa."

She felt some kind of spasmodic contraction throughout her body. She controlled her shivery right hand with the other and opened the file of Mariam, on the computer.

Maryam Isa: Female

Nationality: Egyptian

D.O.B.: 26-01-2017

The same birth day of Sneha's daughter. Maryam was also born in the same hospital where Sneha gave birth to her daughter. She recalled those days in the hospital, six years back. The memory of the blue-eyed Egyptian beauty came into her mind. That lady was screaming loudly because of the pang of child birth. Sneha realized that Maryam is her daughter.

While watching the photo of Maryam on the system, Sneha felt giddiness and found everything around her revolving. These are the blue-eyes, which she saw, a while ago.

"There will certainly be a case against the guardian for the lack of proper attention." Those words of Anupama echoed in Sneha's ears.

"No, it's not carelessness. It was sheer murder. That man killed both the child and her mother. That wicked man! Her mind repeatedly said it aloud.

Sneha recalled her going near to that Egyptian beauty's bed to bid goodbye, on the discharge day from the hospital. They both had the delivery on the same day, and she was also discharged along with Sneha. The newborn was very tiny, and she looked at her fondly. She bid goodbye, saying "See you again", lovingly. All these instances flashed through her mind.

"Baby, there was an Aunty, adjacent to my bed in the hospital who delivered a baby girl like you on the same day, at the same time.", Sneha used to tell this very often to her daughter. Also, whenever she used to pray for the health and happiness of her daughter, Sneha used to pray the same for the other girl too, though she was somewhere else.

Maybe, it will be Maryam's mother herself who sent Maryam to me. She might have longed for somebody to know about the reason for her death. Moreover, she might also have thought that there won't be any other fit person than me, to pray for Maryam to reach her mother's place.

"Oh dear daughter, why did you come to me? Why did you put me in such a dilemma, which will haunt me throughout my life? I had actually prayed for your mother to come near to you, in your dream. I never wanted you to leave this world. I will firmly believe that you have reached your mom forever. Based on that belief, I will cross this ocean of sorrow. I will console myself that you are in the heaven, because heaven is the abode of your mother."

With a heavy heart and wiping out the tears often, Sneha prepared the medical report of Maryam Isa, based on the doctor's notes. Just an entrustment, directed by God!

Benevolence

"Vanamalee Gadee Sharangee shanghee, chakree cha namdakee."

"Sreemannarayano vishnurwasudevobhi rakshathu".

Hearing this verse from Vishnu Sahasranama, Jayachandran approached his wife Hema who was cooking in the kitchen.

They themselves feel that the Vishnu Sahasranama that they hear every morning from Hema's mobile in the kitchen brings a positive energy to their Dubai flat, as if the Lord extends a helping hand during tough times.

"Dear", Jayan called Hema.

"Are you not yet ready to go? It's already seven. I too have to reach the office by nine. Um…m, what happened to you? You look a little bit dull…?", Hema looked at Jayan and asked.

"Hema, you know that our Raheem *Bhai is going back from here. Actually he doesn't like to quit working. He wanted to continue for one more year, but the company didn't renew his visa. They justify that he is too old to work, and also not doing his work properly. The actual reasons are not these. The company can hire foreigners in his place for a cheaper salary. There are too many, waiting."

"In any case, bhai must go, why he wants to struggle?". Hema asked.

"Yeah, he must go, but that's not the basis for my grief. Once, a machine, which was not that old, got some defects and Raheem bhai tried to repair it. He was confident about it, because he is such an experienced person, but, unfortunately, the machine got completely damaged and non-functional. The company authorities put all the liabilities on his shoulders. So, he was compelled to repay a large sum from his settlement agreement. In fact he did that job with good intention. The officials were supposed to consider his service and age, but the company's intention was to tax from him the maximum and to let him go. From the settlement amount, they cut three thousand dirhams, which is a large chunk. That too out of twenty years of service! Raheem bhai came here four years before me. He used to be a tailor in the company. Subsequently, the company entrusted him other jobs. It was bhai who stitched the company uniform for me, during the past years. If we trace back our life, we two were sailing in the same boat. I don't have any kind of savings, bhai too didn't amass anything."

"Is this something new? I know all these factors and I don't think this is your actual problem now, tell me what is in your mind".

"Since I was handling the accounts, I was unknowingly a participant in that salary cutting. Shall I give bhai two hundred dirhams from the money set aside to be transferred in the account for the rent of the flat next week?".

"Even if you were not involved in this matter, would you abstain from giving some amount personally to bhai?".

"No, never. I would certainly. Even then……"

"What even then? Do you have to ask me to do whatever you like?".

"No, you know that the money for repaying the flat rent was adjusted by taking much efforts. If we give two hundred dirhams to bhai now, we have to find it within one week and you often ask me "will you get money by digging the earth"!?"

"You too know that those words are too casual. Anyway we have got one week for remitting the rent. In between, somehow we can arrange. You give bhai from our saving. We can feel happy that even with all these burdens on our shoulders we were able to do something for our beloved bhai. That will bring us a lot of comforts, and we can have peace of mind too. This life is meant for doing benevolent services to others. Now, certainly we can give the amount to him. The other options, God may show us!"

Jayan moved close to Hema, and hugged her.

During lunch break, Jayan saw Raheem bhai in the pantry. He was standing there and looking out through glass window, and was watching the vehicles moving through the streets of Dubai, in the melting heat.

"What is there, this much to ponder over, bhai? You will reach home, within one week." Jayan put his hands on his shoulders and said.

"Oh, nothing Jayan. I started my gulf career here only. Certainly, it is quite natural to have some pain while leaving such a place. I was thinking about that. It's really a pleasant thing to stay at our home country. I really wanted to arrange the marriage of Muneera. That's why I tried for the extension. But they didn't allow me! So far I did a whole lot of things for my people. All my younger siblings are married now. Built a small house, but, when the case of my daughter became inevitable, I lost my job…. It's okay, maybe God will show another way."

"I came to know that they will cut some amount from your benefits. I feel a little bit disturbed."

"That doesn't matter Jayan, I expected more from them. They are the people who cut my two weeks' salary when I was affected by COVID. I would be the happiest person in this world if God expand their burial ground as a reward for cutting my 3000 Dirhams." Bhai said with a smile, while his eyes were wet! He continued: "let things be like that. What's your plan? When you arrived here, I had the belief that you would start your own business and will prosper. Also, it was my great wish to have a job in your company. It never happened. You never saved. You just gave people, even if you don't have in your hands. You never exploited your abilities. I will evaluate you in this way only. I still feel sad about you. Jayan, you still have opportunities. Hope, you may remember my telling you that you are not a person to waste your life here."

"I don't want anything bhai. My home country has been calling my mind and body for a while, I am missing my village, home, father, mother, siblings. I should go soon, leaving everything. I am really fed up, sometimes I think my heart can't bear the workload."

Saying these, Jayan took two hundred dirhams from his pocket and kept it in the hands of Raheem bhai and held their palms together.

"I only have this much to give."

"What's this Jayan?, I don't want this. It's true that I am a man plunged in domestic troubles, but my hands will get burned if I take this money from a man who sails in the same boat, as I do." Bhai tried to return it to Jayan.

"Bhai, if you don't take this money, my mind will only burn and that will never heal. Always Hema used to say that the pleasure lies in giving, that's why I was not able to earn money as you said, but I was successful in achieving love, which you shower on me and to me those are the invaluable savings. When you take this money, I will be the happiest." He held his hands more tightly.

Both bhai's and Jayan's eyes filled with tears. They were in a haste to overflow!

"When you go back, don't forget to make calls to inform about special news off and on bhai."

"How can I abstain from calling? Especially, you. My intimate relations are here only."

Raheem bhai took a cover and handed it over to Jayan.

"You keep this, these are the uniforms for you for the coming three years. There is one colour shirt and a small frock for your daughter. No need to reiterate that I only stitched them. You have never changed in the matters of height and weight, so there was no need of measurement. I have stitched them according to your likings. As Hema mentioned, giving always makes us happy and that need not be money all the time."

Handing over the packet, bhai patted on Jayan's shoulder, hugged him and walked away.

Jayan held that dress packet near to his chest. He was quite sure about one thing that bhai has moved from there with great sorrow and tiredness based on the firm belief that he didn't receive the deserving benefits for his selfless services for the last many years.

Actually, Jayan did not have any kind of involvement in cutting the salary of Raheem but he was sure that all those who are waiting in the queue to step down will have to bear the burden of that sin in future also. Jayan was also convinced that the most experienced person in that queue also will have the same fate.

Jayan recalled the last verse in the Vishnusahasranama.

"Kayena vaacha, Manasindriyairwa, budhyatmanava prakrithe swabhavath!

Karomiyadyal sakalam parasmai, Narayanayethi samarpayami (Oh, Lord Krishna, whatever I do is not with my awareness, I surrender everything on your feet.)

*Bhai - Brother

A Treasured Relation

Nithin was in deep slumber, enjoying the holiday on a Friday. The ongoing ringing of his mobile woke him up. It was only seven in the morning. "Who is calling at these early hours?", he thought indolently and took the phone and his colleague Shabeer's name was displayed in the screen.

"Hi, Shabee, what's up, early in the morning?"

"Hi, Nithin….." Nithin realized the stumbling in his voice.

"Tell me Shabeer.".

"Nithin, ….our Josettan* ….left us…".

"What, Josettan left? Where did he go? He called and talked to me last night. Then where can he go, all of a sudden?".

"Dear, Josettan went to bed and didn't wake up. He had a cardiac arrest. He left us, …Josettan left us." Shabeer was weeping at the other end.

Nithin threw his mobile on the bed and sat tiredly in a benumbed state. He was shocked about the sudden departure of Josettan and he wanted to scream.

Joseph Chacko Peruvayal, was a native of Kozhikode, a place in Kerala. For all of them he was Josettan. He was the person who received Nithin when he first arrived in Sharjah Airport, twelve years ago. He was twenty four then. Josettan was the P.R.O. in the company and their relationship began from that moment.

"I am Joseph, from Calicut. Everybody call me Josettan. You are from Trivandrum, isn't it? It will be twenty two years this December since I moved to UAE. I came here at your age. Each year, I think of going back home the next year, but, Nithi, it never happens. Hope, you never mind me calling Nithi, do you?

"No problem, Josetta!"

Actually, I got surrendered before his affection at that very particular moment itself. He used to call me, "Nithi" with lots of love in his tone.

Whenever he returns from home, he used to bring fried beef, dry chutney, salted and dried veggies, special sweets of Calicut and so on. He got it prepared by his wife Celina. Whenever Nithin wanted to go to the airport, Josettan only took him and he only brought him back. In the case of Josettan, this was vice-versa. Both of them had established it as a right.

When Nithin goes to airport to receive him, Josettan will hand over all the items brought for him before entering the car. "Nithi, you keep all this in your room. When everybody come to my room and begin to snatch, you won't be getting anything".

After four years, Nithin joined in another company, which was much better than this one, as regards salary and other perks. Even then, his relationship with Josettan got more strengthened.

Josettan has got a boy and a girl. Last year, his daughter got married. When Nithin came here for the first time, Josettan's daughter was twelve and son was eight years old. Josettan put an end to his Gulf life and returned home after his daughter's marriage, but he was not able to manage the wedding expenses according to his plans. It all went beyond his calculations.

Then he gave a call to Nithin," Nithi, once again I am thinking of returning to Sharjah. I can't manage everything here. Even if I stay and work here, I am not at all certain about the years of hard work to repay the debts."

"Is it really needed Josetta?, If you still want to come, do you think that you will be able to go back in two years as you thought? Wouldn't it be better to stay there only?" Nithin asked him.

"It's not our own wish which decides our stay at home, our family also should wish the same way Nithi. Celina is telling that our son is only nineteen now and he has not reached his safe shore yet, so she compels me to stay in Sharjah for two more years. It seems right, when I thought on her suggestion. Also, I contacted my company, and they had agreed to grant me a visa."

"If so, you come Josetta. I will book ticket for you. Just inform me about your convenient date." He used to be all in all to Nithin during the last twelve years.

Nithin lost his dad in his childhood. Josettan was just like a father to Nithin. Sometimes, Josettan acted as his elder brother, or as a friend.

Nithin's sister got married one year after his arrival in Sharjah. His salary limit was not sufficient for applying a loan. Josettan, took a loan on the basis of his salary slip and didn't demand any guarantee from Nithin. Then Josettan told him, "I trust you Nithi, because you too have love towards your family."

His invaluable suggestions helped Nithin a lot during the construction of his new house as well as on the occasion of his marriage. When Nithin was travelling home, for his marriage purpose, Josettan told him: "If my daughter is a little more grown up, I would certainly have arranged her marriage with you, without any consideration about cast or religion." He laughed loudly and continued, "Now I think that I would have got married a little earlier!, ha ..ha. "Anyway, past is past. Your bride to be in every sense is a blessed one. Let God shower his blessings on both of you to have a long and happy married life."

Last year, when he went home for his daughter's marriage, he visited Nithin's house at Trivandrum. Nithin's daughter was eight months old then. On his return to Sharjah, he told Nithin: "Nithi, you are too lucky. Your mum was praising you like anything. Your wife also is a matured girl who adjusts herself in par with your circumstances. Your daughter is just your resemblance, Nithi! When you finish paying the loan installments you took for your marriage, you should go back and live happily with your family. Your mum and wife just wanted you to be there, what more a person working in the Gulf needs?" He then laughed and said, "You know, at my home…nobody takes food without fish or meat. If I stay there, will all this workout?"

"Josetta, I am not going back soon. I am thinking of bringing my wife and daughter here." Nithin replied.

"Don't do foolish things, ok? After two months, you will be freed from the burden of loan here. Never try to renew the loan. Also, do not renew your visa. You go and find a job in Kerala. I am quite sure that you will surely get a job. You are a hard working boy. Dear Nithi, during her old age, who else is there to look after your mother? During the twelfth and thirteenth year of my stay here, I had to catch the next flights on hearing the demises of my father and mom. You will never realize the width and depth of the struggle in the mind till we reach our home. I had that bitter experience too. You never create such a situation by yourself to have such an experience. Let your mom die in your presence. Just take Josettan's words as your father's!"

When they had a get together on Friday, he told, "Nithi, next time when I come to your room, you prepare me a Trivandrum style feast, Boli** and Kheer are a must."

'You just tell me the time, Josetta. Everything will be ready", Nithin said.

Again the phone rang. It is eleven. Nithin was sitting on the bed all these hours, recalling the memories of Josettan. When checked, the call was again from Shabeer.

"Hi Nithee, are you not coming? We are making all arrangements to see off Josettan. Come to the embalming center by four o'clock. One person from the HR department will accompany the body." Nithin didn't reply and cut the phone.

Nithin was supposed to rush and be there as soon as he heard the news, but he couldn't . Josettan is no more, also his loving call "Nithi" will not be there, he thought. His heart felt heavier.

In the evening, Nithin stopped his car very near to the embalming center, at Sonapur. Suddenly, the words of Josettan, echoed in his ears. One day while passing this way in the car, he said: "Nithee, you might have seen, this is the embalming center, but let me say, my wish is to die at home, in Kerala and that too during sleep! Just imagine, how long will I lie cold and frozen in this embalmed box, right?. This time, I came here to stay only for two years. When I go back, I will never return, even if the hill falls down."

A wave of sadness rippled in Nithin's heart, and he made a last ditch effort to stop crying. With stumbling steps, he walked into the center. Shabeer saw him and rushed towards him. All the suppressed emotions burst out and he wept, putting his head on the shoulders of

Shabeer. They stood there for a long time. "You come inside, let's see Josettan", said Shabeer and led Nithin inside.

When opened the box, Nithin saw the same smile on Josettan's face even in his death. Then he said in his mind, believing that Josettan is hearing him: "Is this what you said, you will come for a feast? I have been searching for Boli, in almost all the shops in Sharjah. Were you sure that you will leave us like this, and you said that you will not come back even if the hill falls down? Why did you leave us like this, Josetta? Yesterday night also you warned me, not to take any heavy food during night. You advised me that it is because of this eating style only most of the people, especially in the Gulf region, die in sleep due to cardiac arrest, and you…you only left. I told you, not to come back, but you didn't listen to me. You are now going back, frozen, the way you never liked! I have a lot of complaints about you…Josetta, you go…..but how far…..? Anyway, one day I will also reach you. Then you should give answers for my questions…..we will meet again Josetta and will exchange lots of stories. I am sure you will be waiting for me in another world, on that beautiful shore you always talk about.

"Nithin bowed before the feet of Josettan, turned back and walked away, with a heavy heart. Still the words of Josettan echoed in his ears: "Nithi, you should not renew your visa next year and you should go back to your home country when you finish paying the loan dues. Live happily with your mom, wife and child with whatever income you get there. Please do not spoil your youth in this desert."

"No, Josetta, I will certainly follow your words. Next year, I will quit my job and go back home. I can't continue here with your memories, without your presence. I will arrange a feast, added with Boli and Kheer, during the annual rites in commemoration to you. I will continue this offer, till my death. I am pretty sure that you will come to have it". Nithin said these words to himself.

A breeze gently caressed on his face and passed! That breeze carried the same smell of the perfume which Josettan was using in his daily life!

*Josettan – Elder brother.

**Boli – A sweet made with besan flour.

A Woman's Life

"Is Abhishek Sir, here?"

Constable Shiva, turned his head towards the questioner.

He saw a hollow – eyed woman with a tired face, wearing a faded blue saree, modestly, standing there. She had a purse and a small cover in her hand and twiddled it. Shiva recognized that lady, after a second look. She is the mother of Vineeth, who committed suicide, two weeks ago. They live two houses away from the Police Station.

"Sir is not here. He is on a tour. It will take two more days for his return. Do you want to tell him something?"

"When Sir comes, can you give this to him?. Please tell him that Vineeth's mother gave this." She handed over the sealed cover, addressed to 'Inspector Abhishek'.

Shiva handed over that cover on the third day, when Abhishek reported for duty. It was a brown envelope. Abhishek saw a letter, written in two or three papers, and excitedly, started to read it.

Sir,

I am Malini. Hope you may remember me. I am the mother of Vineeth, who committed suicide two weeks ago. I have put everything in short, as regards to me, and all that I wanted to disclose before you. I request you to read it.

My father was an ordinary wage-laborer. He used to look after the family. Daily after work, he came back home after consuming liquor. He used to scold and assault my mother, me, and two of my younger sisters. We never had a pleasant childhood. We were afraid during the nights, awaiting father's assault as well as use of foul language. When I was sixteen, he died in a motor vehicle accident. Truly, dear Sir, we began to sleep peacefully, after that!

My mother arranged my marriage, before I got seventeen years, to a middle-aged man, who was a painter. I can't blame my mother. She wanted to marry away my other two sisters too. I too was convinced with that aged man, hoping that he would love me more, and my future life will be fine.

Unfortunately, everything went upside down. My husband's behavior was more vigorous than that of my father and went to its extreme. He used to drink, smoke, and was always agitated. He scolded and assaulted me. Moreover, association with other women. At the same time, he was suspicious about my character. I spent my life span of twenty years with him after the marriage. I suffered a lot, Sir. He used to punish me too. He made me stand on my knees, that too without any dress, till dawn. Sometimes, I felt severe aching, and even bled. He never had a soft corner even if I cried loudly.

I suffered all these for the sake of my son, Sir. It was all my infatuation that if I get my son well educated, he may reach heights, and finally I can lead a happy and peaceful life. So, I tolerated everything. I couldn't escape from that vicious circle. I had nowhere to go. If I go to my mother, it will become a burden again to her, so I didn't attempt. My husband never allowed me to continue for more than one day in the work places, which I myself found out. He used to come there, create problems, and take me back along with him. He succumbed to hepatitis due to over consumption of liquor, and died two years back.

Afterwards, I worked as a house-maid, and lived for my son, Sir. I worked in almost all houses around here, as a part of my efforts to make my son in high status but his behavior was just opposite to my expectations. He put them all upside down. He had the same character shades of his father.

He used to look at me suspiciously as his father did. He used to talk like that. He became alcoholic, used drugs, and made quarrels. Once he had beaten me also. He used to throw things outside. I tried my level best to correct him, but, literally I failed in that matter, as happened, miserably, in the case of his father.

One week before his death, he told, he never liked going for studies, also, he has got a love affair, and he is going to bring that girl to our home. I felt like falling directly into burning fire, from the frying-pan. I just imagined about his future deeds towards that girl, comparing twenty years of my experiences, I suffered from his father. I never wished to see another innocent girl undergoing such bitter experiences.

I myself, his own mother, put Zinc Phosphide* in his food, to avoid such a fate to that innocent girl. He came senseless because of overdose of liquor, and was not able to find out the difference in taste of the food. First, I thought of having the same food with him and die along with him. Instantly, I changed my mind, for I wished to sleep peacefully, just for one day, at least.

I never had regrets in my actions. I may be considered as a culprit in front of our legal system, but I will surely get a bail in the court of God.

When you finish reading this, I know that you will come here to arrest me. I will be here only, waiting for your arrival.

Malini.

Abhishek put the letter into the cover and sighed. He walked towards Malini's house, putting the letter in his pocket.

When Malini saw Abhishek, she locked her house, and was ready to go with him. She said, "Come, let's go, Sir."

Abhishek handed the brown envelope to Malini.

"Vineeth's mother, you hold this. Since your house is very near to the police station, I know some of your stories. Mom, you too know that I have warned Vineeth, many a times. Let's consider this as his fate. You never gave me this letter, and I never read it. You just burn it now itself."

"Many of the crooked criminals had escaped from my own hands. You did this for your survival. God may delete some of my wrongdoings from his account book, if I close my eyes towards your guilt, I hope."

"Mom, now onwards, you should live peacefully, as you wish. Even in the midnight, you can come to us, whenever you need a help. We are there, very next to you, for your service." Saying these, Abhishek turned back and walked away.

Malini's eyes were filled with tears. Was it right, what Abhishek Sir did? Or Was it right on her part to keep silent? Did she commit a mistake? Malini stood there, unable to define the situation. The enwrapped brown envelope got soaked in the hot tears!

*Zinc Phosphide = Rat Poison

The Mask

"Rakhi, you get sleep only if you go there and sleep? What's the problem with you in sleeping here? Remember that you are a grown up girl now. How many times I have to remind this girl? What can I do, other than this blabbering?"

Rakhi's mother asked her, when she was preparing to go to her aunt's house, just the adjacent neighborhood to sleep.

"There I can have a pleasant sleep. The bed there is a fine one. Here, I have to sleep on the floor, just on a sheet. Also, the fan works well there. Our fan always rumbles, and always breaks the sleep. I have been telling you to replace the fan here and always your reply is there is no money. Also, even if I keep my ears closed with two fingers, the snoring of dad will make disturbance."

"You talkative preacher, shut your mouth. You should learn to live with the limited resources we have and also should learn to suffer the troubles. You are now fourteen. It is high time to stop your sleeping at other's house. Do you really think that they like your sleeping there? They keep silent, only for the sake of our kinship."

"So what, I do stay in Renu's room. She has a separate room for her. I never sleep with uncle and aunt in their room. Here, we only got a single room for three of us. I like sleeping there." She replied blatantly.

"Denying my advices and disobeying is your practice. You should learn to listen to your mother. You always have your own justifications to substantiate your decisions. You carry on as you wish. You keep going there till they ask you to stop sleeping there. You are now big enough and I don't want to give you any physical punishments. I am telling all these for your benefit. Not only in this matter but in everything you do. Later you shouldn't regret and feel sorry for your deeds."

"What is this much serious issue in me sleeping there? I sleep there and comes back early in the morning. That's it. I am going, otherwise they will close the doors.". Rakhi didn't listen to her mother and ran to the adjacent house.

Rakhi's aunt's house was just opposite to their gate. It is a double storied building. Rakhi always used to compare her three–room, non-painted house with that one.

"How beautiful is Renu's house! She is so lucky. Would I have a house like this anytime?" Renu is one year elder than Rakhi, but she called her Renu.

Rakhi discarding her mother's protest, daily went to her aunt's house to sleep. Her aunt, in fact was not happy with this practice. Renu took a neutral position in this regard. She never said yes or no to Rakhi. But her uncle seemed to be very happy. During daytime, when they met, he used to tell her "Rakhi, you come and sleep here, ok!?" This invite, Rakhi liked very much and she felt happy. Rakhi believed that the happiness in life is based on these sort of comforts.

Rakhi felt much annoyed when she saw Renu's father pampering her on many occasions. Rakhi also is the only daughter to her parents. But her father is always very adamant. He used to call her, Rakhi, instead of 'dear'. But her uncle used to call Renu, 'dear' always. That's why Rakhi got the deep rooted belief that Renu is very fortunate.

Renu's room was on the upstairs. Her parents slept on the ground floor. Rakhi's aunt never allowed Renu to lock her room.

As usual, Rakhi went there to sleep. She fell asleep, all of a sudden. At some point of time, she felt something crawling on her body. She saw clearly in the moonlight that came inside through the windows, her uncle keeping one hand on her chest and the other in between her legs, looking longingly at the place where his hands were placed. A terrible shudder took over her mind but someone inside told her to behave calmly and she coughed a little and rolled over herself to the other side. Renu was in deep sleep beside her, not aware of any of these instances. She gave a pry look and saw her uncle fleeing from that room hurriedly.

She couldn't sleep the whole night, not even able to close her eyes. She was in a state of numbness, and was not able to believe what she saw and experienced. She felt feverish. She considered him as her own father, a homely person in front of all the family members and being loved by everybody. Most of her relatives, in public or privately, used to say that everybody should learn from him how to care for the family. She lay on the bed, thinking about the behavior of her uncle, with a frozen mind. With a shiver, she grasped that he is having an evil mind behind his sweet coated words. He used to call her for sweeping and cleaning the front yard occasionally. He used to stay there staring at her till she finishes the job. When she did the work in a stooping position, his eyes might be certainly focusing on her body. That thought brought in her a kind of disgust towards him. Throughout the night she thought a lot and somehow managed till the dawn. When the rays of sunlight began to spread, she opened the front door, came out, closed it, and went to her own house.

She couldn't face her mother and put a sheet on the floor and lied on it. Her hot body started to cool down then. When she was falling into sleep, she heard her mother asking mockingly, "Are you still sleeping on your ornamental cot?, If you again go to sleep, when will you go to school?"

"I am not going to school today, feeling severe headache. Let me sleep." She said in a sleepy mood.

She did not tell anyone what had happened, some truths should not be revealed, sometimes no one would believe her, and if she did, the impact would be worse than an earthquake and she should not destroy relationships.

Rakhi was surprised, mom says that she is not mature at all, but how could she think so maturely in this matter.

That night, instead of going to aunt's house, Rakhi started sleeping in their room on a sheet, "Why?, aren't you going there?" her mother asked.

"No, I'm going to sleep here only."

"Um…m…What happened to think so?…To take a self decision not to go there and to sleep here?"

"There's been a terrible cockroach problem for a few days. A huge cockroach flew in while I was sleeping and bit my legs. Mom knows no that I'm afraid of cockroaches?, So, now onwards, I will sleep here only."

"That's really funny. In order to obey your mother, you needed the bite of a cockroach! Anyway, that's fine. Girls must sleep in their homes only. Ok, I will close the door and come back."

Meanwhile, Rakhi heard uncle asking, "Rakhi, is not she coming?", standing at the gate. Then my mother replied innocently, "She will sleep here only, Renu's dad." Rakhi felt simultaneously, anger, disgust, and hatred towards the inquirer and love and sorrow towards the person who answered!

If she had followed her mother's advice earlier, she would not have to feel sorry as now, Rakhi thought. It has become a truth in her case, that those who neglect the advices of mother, they will certainly have to regret in future. In real life, though Rakhi's father and mother do not express their love explicitly, this house is the heaven and most secured place for her.

She never needed, at that moment, to ponder over the sort of love her uncle was showing towards Renu. She realized that she has no role in deciding the kind of that love, in whatever way it being manifested.

She now is convinced firmly that all luck and misfortunes in life rely on one factor, and that is 'security', if so, Rakhi is the luckiest in comparison with Renu. But Rakhi could not feel much happiness in her luck, because she had worries about the security that Renu enjoys at her home.

Rakhi stretched her hands and legs and lied on the wide floor, and felt so peaceful while thinking about the unmasking of certain artificial faces. Rakhi never felt disgusted, when she heard the snoring of her father, who was sleeping on the cot.

Years Gone By

I saw that face very clearly in the light of the vehicle, which splashed through, tearing the darkness. It happened while I was returning from the hospital to home in the cab, after my early night duty. When the duty ends at two o'clock, after handing over the duty, normally it will be three thirty in the morning when I reach home. I used to have a nap within that half an hour. Cab driver Vikram, will call out loudly, when the cab reaches at the destination, "Jancy, your stop reached". Vineeth, my husband will be waiting there, carrying our four year old daughter sleeping on his shoulder.

That day, after half of the distance to our destination, Vikram had to apply a sudden break, in order to save a person who crossed our vehicle. The unexpected breaking, made my head to hit on the front seat. I woke up in confusion. I heard the driver rebuking that man who crossed the road. With an anxiety to know what happened to that affected person, I watched on the road, while caressing my forehead.

In that bright light from the vehicle on the opposite side, I saw that face very clearly. That figure looked like a disgusting one with scattered hair, without a shower for many days. I got shocked to see the lengthy scar on his forehead and half wounded left eyebrow, but I put that figure in my mind as a framed photo.

"It seems he is a deaf and dumb person. He shows some gestures.". Driver Vikram moved him to the margin of the road and returned to the cab. I wanted to see that face once again and I tried, but due to the darkness on that side, I just saw a shadow figure.

Getting out at my destination, I took the baby from Vineeth's shoulder and entered our flat. After shower, I went to sleep, but the half-cut eyebrow and a face with a long scar on his forehead kept appearing in my mind with a burning in my heart.

Afterwards, whenever I passed along that way, my eyes searched for that face but never saw it. Though occasionally that face came into my mind with the same feel of burning in the heart, in due course I intentionally tried to forget it, because of my workload.

"Sister Jancy, there is one accident case just brought in to the emergency ward. His veins are not available to give injection. The doctor is in search of you, since you being the vein expert. Go fast."

When Sister Shyleena came and told me this, I just closed the file of the patient which I was writing and walked fast to the emergency ward, where the patient was admitted. I examined him and found the vein and when I was trying to put the canula, I just glanced at his face. I got shocked! It was the very same person who met with the accident on that day having lengthy scar on his forehead and a half wounded left eyebrow.

"Some vehicle hit him. But it drove away. Somebody from the mob, brought him here. There is wound on the forehead and fractures in hand and leg." Though I heard the doctor saying all these, I was still staring at that unconscious man.

"Jancy, you should take care of this patient. Should give much care to him. The persons who brought him here told that he has derangement of mind. It seems that there is nobody to look after him. If no one comes and enquires about him, we can shift him to the Government Rehabilitation Centre."

I listened to the advice of the doctor very happily and started my duties earnestly. Though hesitated for a while about his name to be noted in the file, I wrote "Jaison" instinctively.

My elder brother Jaison was three years elder to me. My parents used to call him, Jayasappa. I used to call him, Jayachacha. He was born with certain genetic handicaps. He could only speak very few words, that too by cutting those words into simple syllables. He called my father as, Ap…cha, and mother as, Am…chi and called me as Ja……si.

Jaychachan was a very loving person. Though he has got a whole lot of disabilities, he never disturbed anybody. Many people described him as mentally retarded but, for us he was all in all. We never hurt him even using a single word or look, he, in turn too!

Whatever things he got, he used to keep a share for me, saying "for Ja…si too". He loved me so much. He used to sleep in between my mother and father, hugging them.

When I was eleven years old, we missed him. Sitting on our door step, he was playing with a toy horse, which he liked very much. My mother was busy cooking in the kitchen. After a while, when she came out and looked for him, he was not there. The toy horse was lying there lonely, ownerless!

We searched for him everywhere, local as well as distant places, for a long time, but we never got him back. Many people searched for him on railway lines, ponds, and on sea-sides. We never availed any information about him.

Some of our close relatives tried to convince my parents. "Actually, God helped you to come out of the troubles related to his care taking. So relax yourselves." Since then, my father never allowed those people even to enter our yard. My parents used to weep all the time, in his remembrance.

"Did, my Jaisappan eat something? Who will feed him when he is hungry? Where might he be sleeping? Asking such questions on their own, they cried loudly. In this way, somehow, they continued their life. After my marriage, when my daughter was born, I found my parents becoming a little bit happy and laughing. Many a times I compelled them to stay with me for some days, I suggested them to appoint a care taker to look after our house at Kottayam, but, they avoided my request by reciprocating as follows: "When Jayasappan comes, he will be unhappy if we are not present here, so we are not coming anywhere." They waited for Jaichachan's arrival, each day.

It has been sixteen years, two months and eight days since he went missing, a number memorized by the three of us. He was fourteen years old, when he disappeared. Jaichachan also has his left eyebrow cut in two, he also had a long scar on his forehead. When we were young, I took the sickle, without my mother's notice, and played with him. Unexpectedly, the sickle hit on his forehead and he got an injury. Thus he got the scar, even the wound got healed. My mother was very angry and started to beat me severely. He stopped mother from doing so by saying: "Ja……sy

…..is…inno……cent, mom, please do…not…b…ea…t…j..aa..sy." Even now, those words resonate in my ears.

I got too much inspired by the thought that this patient could be my Jaichachan. I did the best services for him. When he recovered a lot and was able to sit, I cut his long hair and shaved off his beard. I cleaned his body with warm water. Shockingly, yet happily I could recognize my elder brother's face in his childhood. I prayed to the Almighty all the time, that he should be my own brother. In order to make him understand me, I often called him, "Jaichacha". In between, I told him that " I am "Ja…..sy," but there was no response.

During the following days, once I brought my daughter to the hospital for vaccination, I took her to his room. When he saw her, he called her "Ja…si,…..Ja…si." I started to cry loudly, confirming that the patient is none other than my missing brother, "Jaichachan." I hugged him and gave him a lot of kisses. I didn't care about the people who surrounded there, hearing my cries.

"Where were you all these days, Achacha? We looked for you, everywhere. Do you know how much our mom and dad cried? I too cried. I am your Ja…si, Achacha. You shouldn't go anywhere, You know, since how long mom and dad are waiting for your arrival? How many years, have they been waiting?.

He turned his head against me. He rejected my hugs and kisses with one hand. As the replies to my questions, he looked at my daughter and called out "Ja….si, Ja…..si, …..Co….me." He recognized me as the little girl in my childhood, through my daughter. I didn't feel sad about it. I really forgot myself, when I got back my brother. Actually, I wished to know, what happened to him during all these years. But I left those wish as such, since the reunion was really an accomplishment in my life.

The very same day, I made arrangements to bring my father and mother to Mangalore, by sending Vineeth. I particularly asked Vineeth, not to disclose the news of our reunion to them. I eagerly waited for their arrival with rapid heartbeats! Let them arrive and see him directly, I thought.

When my parents arrived, they saw him, calling them, uttering "Ap….cha….., and Am…..chi". My parents began to cry loudly and said. "Oh, Almighty, You are great. Before calling us to your abode, you gave back our son. Jaisappa, where were you our dear! All these years, we were in fire." They, sat on each side of him, hugged and kissed him. In low voice, cried and whimpered to shed off the miseries they suffered in the past, pertaining to the separation, in its width and depth. Meanwhile, they prayed to the God. Then my brother, looking at my daughter, uttered, "Ja….si,….. Ja….si,……come!" I entered into that circle of protection!, my heaven!, with my daughter. At that moment, I was praying to the Almighty to provide the hand support of my parents and brother to me for a long time.

Unity in Diversity

While I was working as a medical transcriptionist in a B.P.O. Company at TechnoPark, Trivandrum, I never thought of doing the same job, after my marriage, in the same sector at a hospital in U.A.E. I joined there as Medical Secretary, in the I.C.U/N.I.C.U in 2016. The security in that unit was Khadeeja, an Ugandan lady. We became very close friends, soon. She told me about her peaceful, beautiful country and the Malayalee industrialists there. During the leisure time, I too described about our beautiful, lush green, God's own country, Kerala.

I used to tell stories about waking up early in the morning, preparing the breakfast and meals along with dishes. Meanwhile, Khadeeja in a surprise mood, will ask, "Shuhaada (What is this?), Why do you cook like this, Mahi? Cook less. Eat bread, sandwich, or Zaatar and sleep more. You are wasting your energy, Mahi. You should love yourself."

Then I will start thinking about the hazards of cooking. We Malayalees, are the only people struggling for cooking. We spend most of our time for cooking, washing and cleaning. Can we think about another lifestyle? It's doubtful. Sometimes, I shared her the food which I prepared. Then she said:

"Um…m.. now I can understand, why you people cook like this. It's very tasty, Mahi."

I firmly believe that we like to hear positive comments from the people who eat our food, in turn fill our minds with happiness. Khadeeja and I worked together only for six months, still, she is one of my best friends.

The only hurting thing while working in the I.C.U. was the death of patients, and shifting of those bodies. I still remember the day when I saw the shifting of a dead body, from ICU, for the first time.

After that, I used to pray to God there shouldn't be any dead body shift during my duty time.

Khadeeja and I continued to tell stories. also used to chat with her daughter who stays at her sister's house in Uganda. On certain occasions, we quarreled each other. Sometimes, we felt sorry for the patients and prayed for them.

One day, a Pakistani youth, aged 35, was admitted due to cardiac arrest. The bystander with him was his slim, beautiful wife, Thayeeba. She seemed tired, because of crying. They got married 5 years ago and no kids, still their life went on very happily. That morning also, he left home for work after bidding goodbye to her. On the way, he had the cardiac arrest, which affected his brain. There was nobody to support Thayeeba. So we supported her. Also, prayed for her better half.

He was in coma, because of brain death. Whenever she comes out of his room, Thayeeba told, "I know, he will come back. He knows that I can't live without him." Within two days, her parents arrived from Pakistan and she has got companions.

While Thayeeba's husband was undergoing dialysis due to the kidney failure, she requested to stop the dialysis. She told the doctor that although he is in coma, she could recognize the pain which he can't suffer. I wondered if it could be true that someone in coma can be aware of his/her own pain.

In the midst of her sufferings, Thayeeba told us the stories about them, showed us their photos, and told about her younger sisters, who were studying in Pakistan.

Within a short while, on a scorching summer day, her husband passed away. I still remember the day me and Khadeeja wept at the thought of Thayeeba's future life, as if it happened yesterday. She didn't give up, she hugged us with tears and said, "You both gave me strength, you cried with me, I can never forget you both till I am alive, we will meet again". I still search for Thayeeba's face from among the mob on the streets in U.A.E. She was standing in the middle of her father and mother, inside the lift, when we last met. We looked at each other, till the elevator door got closed. We never heard about Thayeeba after she returned to her home country.

Whenever I hear the name of Pakistan, the memories of Thayeeba will come to my mind. I never thought of Pakistan as our hostile country. I think that unity in diversity gets an in-depth meaning in the Gulf countries, where people live together in harmony. There is no hostile country or no friendly country, here all are equal. Let me convey my heartfelt love and prayers to my colleagues and neighbors from Uganda, Pakistan, Sudan, Jordan, Philippines, Egypt, Sri Lanka, Nepal and so on.

Son (Son in Law)

"Doctor, today is the 22nd. There are only three days left, excluding today, for the marriage of my younger sister, and that is on 26th. Hope, nothing will happen to father before the marriage ceremony as he is in the ventilator."

I asked the pulmonologist like a stupid. Hari, my husband, was sitting near to me, but he didn't say anything, nor he didn't ask anything to the doctor. He held his fingers together and fixed his eyes upon them.

"See, Miss. Anjali, your father's lungs are affected by cancer. When the lungs stop functioning, he needs ventilator support. It is hundred percent mechanical, but it is not a machine meant for holding his life forever. We can't do anything when the heart stops functioning, that means a fully ventilated person can have cardiac arrest at any moment. No need for me to tell what happens next!"

'Ok, doctor, tell me more. Anyway, father is in the ventilator. He needs no outside support. On the day of marriage, we will hire an outsider as his companion, on payment. Will it be enough? How can we spare our time on the marriage day?"

"Then if something happens to your father, is that okay we intimate the bystander than you?" The doctor's words wrapped in contempt and resentment didn't affect my mind. We only know our why and wherefore.

I came for vacation to India from Kuwait, along with Hari after two years to manage and attend my younger sister's marriage. When my father got addicted to alcohol, our mother became our backbone. We didn't have any love or affection towards our father. He too never showed such emotions to us. Our childhood days were much faded due to the alcoholic habit of my father. All our relatives looked down at us in a scornful way because of my father's behavior. He looked at life in a literally irresponsible aspect. Gradually, his addiction to alcohol and smoking increased, and his lungs were affected by cancer, which has aggravated to the third stage, then he stopped alcohol consumption and smoking. He was admitted in the ICU two weeks before. It was exactly on the day before our departure from Kuwait. Even then, I never had any worries about his health conditions. My grievance was about Kunchi my sister's, marriage. Whether we will meet with some kind of hindrance? After all, my world was limited to my mother and Kunchi. I prayed to God all the time, in getting the marriage to be materialized without any problems.

"I will stay here, doctor'. Hari's words broke my thoughts. He didn't wait for me and walked out of the doctor's room. Hari was the second person to love my father with sincerity, other than my mother. My father was lucky in that case, indeed a great luck for him.

Hari was not at all a son in law, but literally, a son to my mother and father. Hari loves my father, as he loves my mother. Only he can do that, which is not possible to me and Kunchi.

I used to call my mother daily but I never enquired about any matters regarding my father or not even mentioned his name by mistake. I just hear what mother tells about him. When mother told about his ailment, I used to reply, "let it be so, it's all he brought upon by himself, let him suffer".

But, Hari used to enquire about him. He called him at least once a day, will ask about food and medicines, whether he had them properly. He will crack some jokes, and they will laugh.

Whenever asked about that, Hari used to tell , "I love your father as I love my own father. From your experiences, you can only behave like this to him. I don't find any fault in it, but I can't consider him as you do. I should never keep him at a distance. Even if I try, I won't be able to do so."

I saw Hari and my father talking, exchanging jokes and laughing together, and I got really surprised, that was just after my marriage, when Hari came to my home twice, before my shift to Kuwait. How fast they became friends and Hari one of my father's favorite? Above all, Hari loved my father as his own. He used to fulfill all his wants, after communicating each other.

When we reached our native place, two weeks ago, father was in the ICU on that day. After two days, he was found a little bit better and was then shifted to the room. On all those three days, Hari only served my father. He put juice in the mouth of my father, drop by drop, because father was not able to chew or swallow hard food. He massaged on his back. Though my father was unable to talk, considering that he can hear, Hari talked to him continuously. He told in father's ears, "Dad, we want to join Kunchi's marriage. You get well soon. Then only we can attend her wedding." Hari pretended to be a palmist and read "Oh, you will live up to ninety". Hearing this my father produced a small smile on his face. When my father got into slumber, he repeatedly called out, "Dad, dad" and brought him out of drowsiness. In fact, Hari nursed my father, better than my mother, tirelessly.

My father didn't utter any of our names, but unclearly made the sounds "HA……..RI" , occasionally.

So, when he told the doctor that he will stay in the hospital, I didn't find it extraordinary.

"How, will it workout, Hari?. You are supposed to act as both the father and brother of Kunchi, during the wedding ceremony. If you stay here, how can we manage? So, your plan won't work out." I went behind him and told.

"The marriage function will go on smoothly. For that there is no need of my presence. But don't you know that somebody must be here? I will stay here till the end of the marriage. Father will certainly look for me during the visiting time. Even if he is in the ventilator, he will be conscious about all the things. You be there for the marriage function and take care of everything. Anyway, we have to manage it. I believe, what I am doing now is the right thing." His words were shivering.

"Whatever happens, the marriage should take place, no matter of postponement at any cost. If we postpone it, mother will not bear it. I too won't. Mine and Kunchi's lives are the sum total of my mother's perseverance in a lifetime, you know that, don't you?", I cried with obstinacy.

"I know everything, Anju, I know. You just calm down. We will arrange the marriage, at any cost. That will happen, but never leave father alone. I will stay here, please." I didn't argue. I held my hands in his tightly and walked towards the visitor's area, and sat there exhaustedly, thinking about Kunchi, and her marriage. Prayed to happen it smoothly. While, Hari leaned on the next seat with his eyes closed.

While the time crawled, I saw Hari waking up shockingly. I asked him, "What happened?".

"Father came here, close to me. Then he told me, 'Hari, I am going dear'. I heard it clearly. Come, we will go there."

He dragged me and ran through the corridor, towards the I.C.U. When we reached there, we saw, two or three doctors rushing into the I.C.U. I heard somebody shouting, "Code Blue, Bed number:3." At that moment, I remembered my father and my heart began to throb strongly. I held Hari's hand and said, "Code Blue, Cardiac Arrest…..our father…"

Hari sat on the floor, and sobbed. The throbbing continued like a kettledrum for half an hour. Then, the doctor came out, and told,

"Sorry, Mr. Hari Prasad, we have tried our level best to resuscitate as per the protocol but he has gone. You can go and see him."

I entered the ICU holding Hari, so he would'nt fall.

On bed number 3, the body of my father lay with it's soul gone.

It was then and only then, that all the suppressed feeling burst forth like mountain water. Of course we will realize the love towards a person only after his death. I held the feet of my father, touched with my forehead and cried as much as I could.

'You don't get disturbed, Our Kunchi's marriage will take place. Tell mother also, but I am going before that. Will see everything from the unseen world." I am supposed to do at least this much for you people, right? Hari is my unborn son, the only doubt is whether I did good deeds to get his love". I heard the words of my father, echoing in my ears, as that from an invisible-being.

At that time, Hari was trying to clean the dried tears in the eyes of my father, with his hands.

My father's body was cremated on the same day, as per the advice of an astrologer. The bones were collected after cremation as part of the obsequies. There was a river near the marriage venue fixed for Kunchi's marriage. The bone ashes were put into the river to flow. Thus Kunchi's marriage took place on the scheduled auspicious moment, and Hari was sure that, our father was nearby, and would watch the marriage function from there.

An unforgivable lie

"Mahi, ma'am said that we should give Rachel a farewell tomorrow, and asked everyone to contribute twenty-five dirhams. When you come tomorrow, don't forget to bring twenty-five dirhams, okay?."

These words that Vidya had told me four and a half years ago hit my ears like thorns. It was the time when even five dirhams were not in our purse, it was the time when trials of god were faced through will power and prayers.

I just shook my head at Vidya's words, also felt sad of not having a single penny. I was wondering how am I going to pay twenty-five dirhams along with everyone else. I did not want to put my husband in pressure, so I never thought of asking him the required money. I walked and left home that day from work with a heavy heart, but gratefully remembering the Lord who enlightens the way even in times of need.

"Daddy, can you give money to put in my piggy bank?.", four-year-old Kunjata (our daughter) asked her father.

"Oh dear, I have one dirham only in hand today, please put it in, will give you more when mom and dad get salary. Please take care of the piggy bank honey, we need it to buy a smart TV." His laughter rang out there.

"Smart TV costs one dirham only dad?". She asked.

"No dear, if we pay one dirham, we will not get smart TV. We have to pay a lot of dirhams, first let this piggy bank gets filled and then we should start filling another one, that's why dad told you to be careful." Kunjata sat on her dad's lap listening carefully to what he was saying. My eyes and intellect narrowed when I saw her putting one dirham in the piggy bank.

As the next day's duty was in the afternoon, after my husband

and daughter left, I took the piggy bank and broke it with a knife. Without any hesitation, I took the twenty-six and a half dirhams that father and daughter kept together for many days. Twenty-five dirhams were also given for the Farewell.

"Dad, please give me two dirhams today, do you have money?", A week later, when Kunjata asked her father this, it was not only my mind got shattered but also my body.

"Daddy have only one dirham today also dear, it doesn't matter, next week I will add and give you three dirhams. Hurry up and put this in, let the small bank fill fast." My mind was in a bad state when I saw her happily jumping and snatching it.

"Daddy, mommy, did you see my piggy bank?, I cannot find it here?", she was on the verge of crying when she went to put the money and returned without seeing the piggy bank. I pretended to be busy in the kitchen. I felt more afraid that my face would not be able to hide the lie.

"Lakshmi, did you see her piggy bank?", he asked.

"How can I see, isn't she the one who is hiding it? Oh…dad's and daughter's piggy bank, if you people cannot find anything, then it will be on my head. I have hundred tasks to do and you are disturbing me asking about silly things." I answered, at the same time I was trying hard to hide my face that was abashed. I prayed to God to forgive me and I believed that he would.

How many nights have I tossed and turned thinking how to remove the guilt of the wrong done, still I think that I would have asked my husband for the money for farewell, he would have arranged from somewhere.

After that, many days, months and years, father and daughter walked in that two-room house searching for the lost piggy bank. Times have changed, circumstances have changed, life has started to take hold, a new piggy bank has come, every now and then more money is falling into it, but still when I see two innocent people searching for the old piggy bank, I, the evil one who robbed them of their savings would say in my mind, "I only took it, don't search for it anymore", with an indescribable sorrow for the wrong deed.

I can't help, requesting your forgiveness I should say this at least through this note.

What might be going through the minds of my husband and daughter when they read this?, will it be that I am a stealer?, untrustworthy?...or a deceiver?, I really don't know, all I know is that I deserve any of these positions.

Lucky

"Hey, Maha, Do you have any idea about my childhood? It was not that pleasant. Though I wished for some things, I never got them. You won't even believe if I reveal some of them."

I was having my lunch. I took a piece of chicken from the lunch box and started to chew it. My colleague, who was having her lunch with me was talking to me. Actually, I thought I was the only one who had a bitter childhood among our group. I had a small bite of the chicken piece and put the rest in the lunch box, "Was her life bitter than mine? Did she live in a poor condition, in comparison with mine?" With much eagerness I asked her.

"What was your trouble?"

"We didn't have a V.C.R. at home. You won't believe. I never saw cartoons on V.C.R. I came to know about cartoon characters through reading books."

"Was this your problem?" I took the returned chicken piece and chewed it hard, as if she didn't have a VCR.

"Why, isn't that a big sadness?, wasn't it in your house?, it was in all my friends' houses." She said again.

"Yeah of course, it's a big shame, I had three VCRs, and when I got tired of one, I'd put another one, so it was such a joy to have a VCR. By the way how did you get all those books?".

"Dad took me to the library in the car, and I borrowed books from there."

She used to have a car and other facilities. Still she was unhappy for not having a V.C.R. How come she got this sort of silly feelings?

"What were your childhood grief then?", her question took me out of my grumbling thoughts against her.

"I didn't have much grief as you suffered. But there were small troubles."

The first among them was the scene of my mother crying as we didn't have rice to cook during our toughest times and even having no money for buying rice. My mother used to think about some alternative measures to feed us."

Two: "Even, while playing with my friends at the neighborhood, my ears and eyes will be vigilant to see whether it is time for my father's arrival or has he reached after consuming liquor? If so, I had to rush home. Because, I had to intervene to stop their quarrelling. Otherwise, my mom will have to suffer physical harassment. Sometimes, I stayed at home, fully abstaining from playing together with my friends, to oversee the actions of my mom with a fear that she may commit suicide to overcome the troubles.

Three: I had the experience of made to stand up in the class for not paying the tuition fee on time, in each term. When my teachers denied me permission for appearing for the examination, I had begged to them, "Mam, please allow me to write the exam, I will certainly bring the fee tomorrow." Also I had lied before them that I had brought the money, but I lost it." This was all to avoid the punishment of standing in the class and to attract the teacher's sympathy. When they realized that I was telling lies, my class teacher pinched on my hand in front of my classmates. I had to bend my head to hide my tears dropping down. I was only eleven then.

Four: One day, my mother asked me to stay at one of my relative's home. The lady served bull's eye to her kids. I was eagerly waiting for that dish. The lady of the household told me: "You do not need bull's eye, do you? I prepared only for them." I told the lady, who was my dad's nearest kin, No, I don't want. I don't like bull's eye." I was only eight or nine years old then.

Five: I was using the same school bag for two or three years and it got torn like anything. My mother told me that she was not going to buy a new school bag that year also. I went to my neighbor's house the next night. They had bought new bags and umbrellas for their kids. I thought that, they might have bought bag for me also. Without any abashment, I asked them, "Where's my bag?". "What? bag for you? Do you think that we don't have any other job? You go and ask your father!", I felt ashamed and I winced. Somehow, I escaped from that embarrassing situation, but I didn't cry. Actually, no tears came in my eyes! I was ten years, then. Whenever, I think about that incident, I still shrink.

Six: Once the electricity department cut out our connection due to non-payment of the accumulated amount, we had managed for many months without electricity. I did my studies in the light of candles, as well as traditional kerosene lamp. We were the only family, in that area, without electricity in the surroundings. I even prayed that it would never be night."

Seven: Once, our water meter, made of iron, was stolen by a thief. We went to the Water Authority office with an application to replace a new one. They told us to remit an amount of Rs.6800 against our water tax dues, then only they would replace the new water meter. My mother didn't even have hundred rupees in her hand. It took nearly six months to clear the dues, that too after borrowing money from many people. Our neighbor, who is one of our relatives, was kind enough and allowed us to fetch water from their tap for our day to day use. The carrying of water in heavy buckets was my duty then. My fingers became swollen. I continued carrying the heavy bucket till the authorities fixed our new water meter. I was in twelfth standard then, I used to carry the buckets of water without even changing my uniform after school. I still remember the struggles I managed during those days.

Eight:……………………

"Why are you staring at me like this? ", she asked me without allowing me to continue.

"Didn't you hear what I ask? What were your troubles during your childhood?"

She didn't hear what I said so far. She will not hear it, because I was recapturing all those incidents in my mind.

"Hey, I didn't have any sorrows as such. I was so happy. I possessed everything." I told her.

"You were so lucky'", she said.

Let it be like that. Let her sorrows be greater than mine. I didn't want to spoil her imagination about me, and finished my lunch.

When I came down from my office space after job, I saw a boy of around twelve years old. He seemed to be a specially-abled boy. When his mother showed him the pictures and lightings, specially arranged for children, they both clapped their hands and laughed. They were not listening to anybody else. They didn't see anything else. They were in their own world! I too started to watch the colorful scenes along with them, laughed and clapped my hands. Two, or three staff members joined with me. Then the boy started to laugh more loudly.

After a while, I bid goodbye to the boy and his mother, by waving my hands. The mother was laughing and happy, though I could see an ocean of sorrows hidden inside. At that moment, I realized the meaning of the words told by my friend, "You were so lucky". I thanked God and said, "I was, and I am lucky".

"If you want to know whether you're lucky or not, go down to the OPD," I decided to tell her that when I go for duty the next day, and I walked out. Behind me, at the hospital reception, the mother and son's cheers continued.

My Neighbour

Hearing the tumultuous noises of children and removal of objects, the arrival of new residents in the neighboring flat was confirmed. As I was eagerly waiting for such an occasion, my heart started throbbing.

"The new residents are from Pakistan", it was my husband Kannan's comment. "I heard Nathur saying that the flat was taken by a Pakistani family. Sudha you should close the door after I leave." The thought that the Pakistanis are alarming, dampened my enthusiasm and even my sleep that day.

Actually I welcomed our move from native place to Abu Dhabi with tremendous joy, however, the thoughts related to the diversity as regards the new place, culture and different people, put me in confusion.

"You needn't go for close acquaintance with other people. Just concentrate on our matters", Kannan always whispered. Basically, I used to be very talkative and friendly to others. Also, I like reading and writing very much. On the other hand, my life partner is just the opposite. He has no friends, talk very precisely, will not laugh loudly, and never cut jokes. Moreover, never touch books at all. He is grave serious all the time. In his looks, during work, on every occasion, he is literally serious. While going outside, I happen to see people resembling Malayalees and I wish to talk to them, but I just glare at them with a beautiful smile and pass by. I started to live in a world with my books. My neighbors arrived at this moment.

I started observing my neighbors through the small peephole of my front door, while they open their door. Opening the door, a little wide, I started watching the two children playing in the corridor. They were very cute girls, aged around three and four years.

"What's your name?", one day I heard this question while

watching the children's play. It was their mother. The root cause of those girls being so cute may not need further explanation. At the first sight of the mother, that became evident.

"Sudakshina", I replied in a little stammering tone.

"I am Fera", she came closer to me and held my hand with a beautiful smile. I felt the coldness of that hand spreading to my body and mind like snow.

I never realized how her fluent English cop with mine, which is literally broken. When I am struggling to find the words to speak in English, I used sign language and sometimes Malayalam. She tried to capture my words without frowning or teasing. We shared everything with each other in our own language as they say friendship has only one language.

In the absence of Kannan, either I spent time there or she spent time here with her children. This has become a routine by now. Everybody used to call me Sudha, as an abbreviation of my name Sudakshina, but Fera in a sweetest tone used to call me Sudhu, and I felt fond of it.

"Sudhu, you know I love Kerala a lot, look how beautiful Kerala is in the photos", one day when Fera said these to me, I struggled to hold my head high, which bowed due to shyness, because I had accumulated many misunderstandings about Pakistanis by hearing accusations made by Kannan, but I miserably failed to do so.

While Fera taught me how to make Pakistani Biryani and its dishes, I taught her how to cook Kerala dishes, especially during feasts and the Fish curry in which Garcinia is used as an ingredient.

Her husband used to stand up and invite me to their house, whenever I visited them. He says, "Sister, please come in", showing due respect. On these sort of occasions, I thought of my husband who used to sit arrogantly with one leg over the other, when visitors come, pretending that he is the superior to all. I felt very sad about his behavior.

Fera taught her kids to call me "Sudhumma". When the kids started to call me Sudhumma, though I am not a mother, my heart get filled with motherhood. When Fera video calls her mother, her mom used to enquire about me very specially. Sometimes, we used to talk for a long time. On such occasions, I forget my sorrow on the memories of my deceased mother.

I felt lonely when they go for vacation. It was on such occasions that I realized that I needed Fera and her friendship more than she needed me and my friendship.

Once, I shared my grief, for not becoming a mother even after four years of married life, Fera consoled me: "Giving birth is not a very important thing in life, Sudhu. It may happen in the due course, but see, God has given you a great gift, the skill in writing. You have to concentrate in it fully and you should publish your own book.". Those words gave me much inspiration.

When God gave me Kannan who did not even read or comment on a single story I wrote, God blessed me enough to give me a neighbor on the other side, who Google translated all the online stories I write and gave valuable opinions as well as greetings.

During one night when Kannan instantly felt dizziness, dazzling of eyes, breathlessness, and chest pain, Fera and her husband immediately brought him to a hospital. The doctors diagnosed and reported that it was due to high blood pressure and he was much lucky to reach the hospital in time, which avoided a stroke. I looked at my neighbors with gratitude. I saw Kannan's eyes also shedding tears.

A drastic change occurred in Kannan's life after that particular event. He wanted to have Fera and her husband in every deeds. He brought numerous toys for the children to play, whom he never wanted to enter our house before. Now he wanted them to play inside our house only. The man who used to abuse them for making disorder inside our house, who not even considered them as innocent kids, now never prevented them from making any kind of disorder. He started buying books for me. Also began reading my stories and started to comment on them. He arranged a special place for me to read and write. We together with the Fera's family, celebrated Vishu, Onam, and Eid festivals in due course, all together as a single family.

Fera and family became part of our life. Fera, is an individual who has indeed imbibed the scripture, "Love your neighbor as yourself".

The first book I wrote, which was titled, "The neighbouring country and the lovely people" was released by Fera. Three years have been passed by then, that book was published in English also for Fera to read.

Yes, this is the woman who brought in drastic change in my life, and she is named Fera, who is the most dearest one to me. She is my neighbor, both in my home country and the bread winning country.

A Letter To My Daughter

"Mahalakshmi, didn't you undergo a major fibroid removal surgery? I called the doctor yesterday as you were a special patient of Dr. Jayakrishnan at KJK Hospital, and he specifically told me not to give you any pain or pressure on the uterus, only to take the child by caesarean section, so we can have a caesarean section. okay?"

I did not have any prior knowledge about normal delivery or caesarean section, but with the knowledge or lack of knowledge that others have said that normal delivery is better, I was waiting on the labour room bed for the pain to come, praying that it would be normal. I lay down and cried for nothing.

While I was crying thinking of cesarean section, the lady in the next bed was crying out of labor pain.

I was surprised when I heard in a half-drowsy state the doctor say, "Lakshmi, it is a baby girl." During my pregnancy, not even a single person said that it would be a girl. Everyone was sure, "It's a baby boy".

"Don't you see the belly?, sure it is a boy."

"You look black and like charcoal, all your beauty is gone. You have a baby boy only, that is why mother is not beautiful at all. If it was a girl, mother would have been beautiful to look at". Not only them who were much sure and more knowledgeable than the creator of all things, but also the confectioner who was assigned to make the fifth month's dessert said, "Yes, it is a baby boy," because the round shape of the desert came or did not come when the flour was poured.

When everyone was so much sure, I also believed that a baby boy was inside my belly. Even when I was praying to God to give me a healthy child, male or female, I used to ask the almighty without any shame, "Lord...can you give priority to the female child".

I don't know if God felt sorry because of my prayer, we were blessed with a baby girl.

The lady in the next bed and I gave birth to baby girls at the same time. I still remember that kid even though I never saw them after that, wherever you are, I will pray for you to be comfortable and happy.

I don't know if it was due to postpartum depression or the stress of having to start working from home within two months of delivery, I had not been able to look after my daughter with much affection and love but I started my office work only after making sure that her needs were attended to on time. Even though there were many people around, I did not receive much help from anyone until she was one year old, thinking that I should not trouble anyone. I can confidently and often proudly say that I am a mother who is different from those who look after their children with a lot of fuss, and those who live thinking that no matter how big their children grow, they cannot take care of them without the help of their own father, mother or anyone else.

When we started living in Sharjah with our daughter at the age of one, more than the joy of being together with my husband, there was more in my mind to organize a job immediately and at the same time the conflict of who would look after her. I was certain that I would get a job, but I was worried about her and God appeared in the form of Mini Aunty to put an end to all those worries.

Mini Aunty who lived in the opposite flat of ours with her husband and younger daughter, took our daughter from us as if it was some kind of ancestral right. Aunty and Uncle, and their youngest daughter, Anna quickly became very dear to us.

Until Anna completed her twelfth standard and they settled in India in April 2018, aunty took care of our daughter like her own granddaughter without expecting anything in return. Aunty always used to say that you are like Arya to me; Arya is Aunty's elder daughter.

That love still remain today, and our daughter still calls Aunty and Uncle as Ammamma and Achacha.

After my mother, I owe the most in life to Mini Aunty and her family. I can't go further with this writing without mentioning Mini Aunty, they are always in our prayers.

It's hard to believe that it was more than nine years ago when I heard "Lakshmi, it is a baby girl", those words are still ringing in my ears like it happened yesterday.

Now my daughter has learned to do almost everything on her own and doesn't need her mother's help for most things. I am not hiding the fact that what a big comfort it is for working mother that I am.

I am a perfectly imperfect mother who scolds her for each and everything and sometimes gives her a good beating despite being a very obedient child. If my mind or body is tired, I vent all my anger on her.

But no matter how much I get angry and my body hurts, the next moment my daughter calls me "mom" with a sweet voice with full of love as if nothing had happened.

When I ask whether she prefers her mother or her best friend father, who to this day has not even scolded her, her innocent and honest reply, "Both", is often hard for me to distinguish whether it makes me happy or guilty.

The rest of this write up is for you dear, you should read them when you can understand them.

Mother has nothing great to say to you. Just a few little things.

Always have a good heart. Whatever position you are in, think as those who are under you and think from other person's side. Even if you don't stand by someone's rise, you should definitely stand by someone's down.

If you see something good, you should appreciate it. Don't blindly trust anyone, not everyone wish for your good.

Respect elders and youngers alike and understand the truth that everyone is different.

Even if you don't always call on your relationships but you feel they're broken, definitely call and be with them. Whatever you do, do it without expecting anything in return, and love with the assurance that even if you love, you will not get love in return.

Control your anger, like dad does.

Don't speak out loud like your mother does, your enemies will be on your list at a young age. Don't hold back on anything because you are a girl, try to do whatever you want.

You need money to live but you should know that the happiness of life is not in money.

If you have something that someone asks you to "give", don't hesitate to give it to the needy, even if it's money. Dear, you should understand that happiness comes from giving and not from receiving.

Study as much as you like, study what you like. Eat your favorite food. Travel as you wish. Life is very short, so enjoy the time you have.

"To get married" should be removed from the priority list of your life. If you feel so in future, accept someone who loves you and also you love, if possible choose someone who loves you more than you love. If you get married, you may be able to live happily with your family, it is not sure. If you don't, you may be able to live happily according to your own choice, you can decide which one you want.

Do what makes you happy, but not at the expense of the other person's happiness. Treat others the way you want them to treat you.

Hold God close to your heart, call out to him when there is trouble or happiness, then he will be there at your call any time. Remember that the path of life will be mostly full of the heat of sun and we have to seek shade ourselves.

Respect all religions and never brag about your own religion to someone who believes in another religion.

When offering food, don't be stingy at all, give generously.

Mom does not say that there should be no jealousy and envy, a girl can be a little jealous, but do not express it openly and do not cross the line.

I believe that there is no need to tell you that all human skin colors are diamond, as you always say that.

Rather than wishing to live long, pray to be healthy and happy as long as you live.

Even though the expectations are heavy, I can't help but hope in you.

No matter what you do, no matter how you live, no matter what difficulties you face in life's journey, as long as your father and mother are alive, you can come to us without a second thought. The door of our hearts and home will always be open for you.

Fragrance of Memories

On a holiday, I took everything from the wardrobe and put on the mat that was spread below, thinking that I could take all the old but good clothes and put them in the charity box. When I took out my husband Hari's old shirts, I saw a brown cover package among them. I picked it up thinking that this was a bundle I had never seen before.

When I opened the package, I saw an old watch. It cannot be said that it is that old, but the watch has started to show all the signs of ageing.

When I took that watch in my hand, I didn't know where it came from, it seemed like some old smell came from somewhere, and very soon that smell went away.   Hari's watches were all on the outer shelf, so I walked up to him with the gold and silver watch with the large dial, wondering whose it would be.

"Whose watch is this Hari? I got it from among your old shirts."

"It's Dad's", he looked at it and took it from my hand.

"How come your Dad's watch be here?"

"It's not my Dad's, It's your Dad's".

"My Dad's?", I asked in a shock.

"Yeah, I bought it during our vacation trip to India, just before his death". "Don't you remember, your mother calling you and asking for the watch?

Yes, mother told me, I recalled.

"Anju, can you bring a watch, especially for your dad, this time? You never gave him anything special since these many years. Usually you used to give everything you brought for others in my hand. I distribute them to all. This time, you certainly should buy one watch for him. That's his great wish. He asked me to tell you".

"Oh, special! That too for him? Mom, can you tell, what special things he did for us? And even if I buy one watch for him, is there any guarantee that he won't sell it and drink alcohol for that money?. I will never buy one for him. You needn't call me again for this purpose. If you need something, you tell me. I will buy and bring it for you".

Hearing my reply, my mother got angry and cut the call instantly. Hari was standing close to me, hearing all these. He glared at me with a mixed emotion, and left the room without saying anything. He is quite certain about the fact that it would be a futile attempt to argue in favor of my father. I am very stubborn and merciless in this matter.

Five years ago, we had a vacation trip back home. Then also I didn't buy anything special for my dad, though I did buy whatever things needed for my mother and my younger brother. Actually my mother imploringly asked me to buy something special for my dad. The next time when we visited home, dad was bedridden. He passed away, after a week.

My memories broke off, when Hari began to talk:

"I fulfilled all the responsibilities due for your father, which were all liable on your part. Though you didn't give anything to your dad, I bought everything he wanted. This watch was bought for him during the last visit. He used to wear it, even when he was bedridden. He never allowed anybody to untie it. Maybe, you might not have noticed it. You never gave any attention to him. It's quite natural that human beings commit mistakes, but when they admit it and regret for the same, we must give them an opportunity to repent.

When he died, I was the only person near to him. I untied this watch and kept it with me. I considered this as a token of his possession. He tied it on his hand the moment I gave it to him and kept it till his last breath. Your mother, once told me "he never keeps this watch away from him Hari, always he wanted to have it with him". I never wanted to neglect this watch which had always been in touch with him and having the fragrance of him".

Hari carefully put that watch into the brown cover and kept it safely in the cupboard. Then he turned back and touched on my shoulders. He continued:

"Till his death, he never knew that it was bought by me. While giving it to him, I told him: "Anju only bought it as a special gift for dad. She entrusted me to give this to you." As he was sure that you will not talk to him, he didn't say anything. He very pleasingly accepted it and held it close to his heart. He carried it with him till his death, considering that it was your gift for him and not because I bought it for him."

After saying this, Hari left the room. I stood there with a half-frozen mind and body. Thinking of something else, I took that watch out. I smelt the same fragrance which I felt when I first took it out. I realized that it was the fragrance of my dad. In my childhood, I used to lie on his shoulders and he used to pamper and fondle me. It was the very same smell! One day my dad was a little bit late to take me back home from school. I started to sob like anything, I was seven or eight years old then, that very memory was more than enough for my eyes to rain again. I held that watch in my hands and put near to my eyes and started to sob, that particular fragrance in my memory still floated around the room.

www.ingramcontent.com/pod-product-compliance
Lightning Source LLC
Chambersburg PA
CBHW051449140726
47987CB00006B/2617